HELEN KELLER
Sketch for a Portrait

BY THE SAME AUTHOR

Published by E. P. DUTTON & CO., INC.

HELEN KELLER

Sketch for a Portrait

BY

VAN WYCK BROOKS ~ 1886

E. P. DUTTON & CO., INC.
New York
1956

CONTENTS

NOTE

The writer wishes to thank the following persons for their kind assistance in the preparation of this book: Miss Polly Thomson, Mrs. Keith Henney, —Nella Braddy,—the author of *Anne Sullivan Macy,* and Miss Helga Lende, the Librarian of the American Foundation for the Blind.

HELEN KELLER
Sketch for a Portrait

I

A CHILD IN ALABAMA

WHEN I was in Saint Augustine in the winter of
1932, Helen Keller appeared at the Cathedral
Lyceum, and I went to see and hear her there, drawn
by curiosity, such as one feels for any world-famous
person. For Helen Keller was not only famous but
she had been so from the age of ten, when she had
sat on the old poet Whittier's knee and Queen Victoria asked Phillips Brooks about her. A ship was
named after her in 1890, and the autocrat of the
breakfast-table, Oliver Wendell Holmes, had published a letter of hers in one of his books. President
Grover Cleveland had received her in the White
House, as other presidents were to do in after years,—
it was known that she had made Calvin Coolidge
smile,—and Mark Twain had said that she was the
most marvellous person of her sex who had existed
on the earth since Joan of Arc. Yet there she was in
Saint Augustine, still young, in 1932, as she was to
remain upwards of twenty years later.

I remember one phrase she uttered then, interpreted by her companion,—for, never having heard
her own voice, she was turbid in speech,—a phrase
referring to the subway in New York that "opened

its jaws like a great beast" which struck me at the moment as reminiscent of the prophets in the Bible. I was not aware then how steeped she was in the language of the Bible, which I later heard her expound with biblical scholars; nor did I know how familiar she was, literally, with the jaws of beasts, for she had once stroked a lion's mouth. The lion, it is true, was young and well fed in advance, but nevertheless she entered its cage boldly, for her "Teacher," as she always called Anne Sullivan, the extraordinary woman who developed her mind, wished her to meet experiences of every sort. Helen had lived as a child on a farm, where she knew cows, mules and horses well; they had eaten apples from her hand and never harmed her; and her teacher, feeling that she should know wild animals as well, introduced her early to the zoo of a circus. She shook hands with a bear, she patted a leopard, she was lifted up to feel the ears of a giraffe. She did not touch the tiger, for the tiger is "wanton," as she said once, an appropriate word but characteristic of a mind that has been fed from books instead of the give and take of ordinary talk. However, she encouraged the elephant to wind its trunk about her neck and big snakes wrapped their coils about her, so that Helen Keller, for this reason partly, grew up without fear, and she remained both physically and morally fearless. Adventurousness and pluck were two of the notes of a life that was to be carried on always in silence, in the dark.

Helen Keller's family lived in northern Alabama, where her father, a Confederate officer who had fought through the Civil War, was a local newspaper editor at the time of her birth. He was in part of Swiss descent, and, as it happened, one of his forbears had written a book on the teaching of the deaf and had been the first teacher of the deaf in Zürich. Helen Keller was equally a child of the South and of Massachusetts, for, while Captain Keller's mother was a second cousin of Robert E. Lee, her own mother was a cousin of Edward Everett Hale. In time the little girl was to see much of the author of *The Man Without a Country*.

Tuscumbia, where the Kellers lived, was a little town of two thousand souls. The sandy roads were lined with blossoming fruit trees and ploughed fields that filled the springtime air with earthy odours, and across the way from the Keller homestead, which was called "Ivy Green," stood an old deserted house of Andrew Jackson. Not far away was Mussel Shoals, later the site of a well-known dam, near Keller's Landing on the Tennessee River, while on every side one still found traces of the old romantic forest that had drawn so many naturalists to Alabama. There the English entomologist Gosse,—Edmund Gosse's father,—had roamed about in rapture with a butterfly net, enchanted by the great hawk-moths that hung in the honeysuckle vines, gorging themselves on the sweetness of the vermilion tubes. Gosse had never dreamed of such blossoms and birds, such larkspurs or such perfumes, or the scarlet cypress vine and the flowering Judas, the pride-of-China trees and the Southern creepers. The buildings, trees and fences of the farm were covered with English ivy, and, with its smokehouse and dairy-room, and with turkeys and pigs, chickens and sheep, the old plantation life went on unchanged there. The Kellers had a summer camp on the top of a mountain as well, where the captain and his cronies gathered for talk and for hunting. There was a wide piazza round it swept by the upland winds with scents of persimmon and evergreen, wild muscadine and ivy; and the elderly Confederates,—Helen's father was twenty years older than her mother,—told tales of their exploits as woodsmen and hunters. The camp shook with the rattling of guns and the heavy footsteps of the men as they strode about at dawn preparing for the hunt, while during the morning when the men were gone the venison or the pig was hung over a pit and turned on a spit for the barbecue at the end of the day.

Helen herself was seven years old before she understood the meaning of any of the life that went on about her. Born in June, 1880, she was a "living nullity," aware only of tactile sensations, vibrations and scents, dwelling in a world, as she wrote later, that was a "no-world," without hope, anticipation, wonder, faith or joy. For, in her aimless dayless life, she was deaf, blind and unable to speak, a small wild animal, violent and stubborn, given to spasms of baffled rage, whose family were often bruised by her assaults. She was a dangerous adversary, as someone put it, whom no one knew how to control, snatching whatever she chose from the dishes on the table and throwing herself in fury on the floor. Presumably normal at birth, she had passed through an illness at eighteen months after which she did not respond to the loud ringing of a bell or close her eyes when her mother dressed or bathed her, although soon, as a child who was legally an idiot, she began to make signs that revealed an intelligence within. She went through the motions of beating batter for a cake and spreading bread with butter after she had cut it. But only meaningless sensations rioted within her, for she was in a state of anarchy, as she was to put it. All she knew was that she was impelled to seek food and warmth, helpless and alone as she was in a deep dark pit. She was to compare herself in these hopeless silent years with a ship groping its way in a dense fog at sea, only she, with beating heart, waiting for something to happen, had no way of knowing that harbours existed. She had, moreover, neither sounding-board nor compass.

But when Helen was six, her mother discovered in Dickens's *American Notes* the account of the education of Laura Bridgman, the pupil of Samuel Gridley Howe at the Perkins Institution, the well-known training-school for the blind in Boston. Laura Bridgman had been the first deaf and blind person in the world who had been taught to communicate with her fellow-creatures, and Dickens, during his American visit of 1842, had written a moving description of this girl and her teacher. There were many stories of the blind who had made their mark in life from Homer down to Saunderson, the mathematician, and the Swiss scientist Huber, the great student of bees, and the education of the blind had been developed widely since Valentin Haüy had opened the first school for them in Paris. That was in 1784, a fruit of the Enlightenment, the movement of intelligence that preceded the French Revolution, like the Abbé de l'Épee's first school for the deaf. But what Dr. Howe called the "disinterring" of the soul of this doubly handicapped girl was something entirely new under the sun, for the "second Prometheus,"—Sydney Smith's phrase,—had rescued her from a darkness and stillness "as profound," he said, "as that of a closed tomb at midnight." This blind deaf-mute's face, Dickens remarked, was "radiant with intelligence and pleasure" as he saw her at the Institution writing her journal, but there was much he did not relate about either Laura or Dr. Howe, who was one of the world's historic teachers. A romantic Bostonian who had fought the Turks on behalf of the Greeks and was later imprisoned in Prussia as a champion of the Poles, he had devoted himself to the blind, written a special geography for them and printed the first atlas with raised maps. At a time when only three books were available for them anywhere, he had started a press that became the most active in the world, and he went about in the Institution blindfolded much of the time to be constantly aware of the obstacles which the blind encountered.

While Dr. Howe had long since died, Laura still lived at the Institution, a proof that something could be done in a case like Helen's, and the Kellers were soon in communication with Dr. Howe's successor, the Greek who had married his daughter, Michael Anagnos. Captain Keller had taken Helen to an oculist in Baltimore, who had urged him to go on to Washington and see Dr. Bell, the inventor of the telephone, Alexander Graham Bell, whose deepest lifelong interest was the teaching of the deaf. A Scottish-American who had lived in Boston as a teacher of the art of speech and who was never happier than when he was teaching,—he had lived for three years with a deaf boy whom he taught to speak,— Bell had invented the telephone as a sort of hy-product of an apparatus to enable his deaf pupils to "see" sounds they could not hear. It was Bell's father who had invented the system of "visible speech" around which Bernard Shaw built one of his plays, *Pygmalion,* in which the diction of the cockney girl was so transformed that she passed for a duchess at a garden party. Bell's own idea was to record the vibrations of the voice visibly on a sheet of soot-covered glass that would indicate the quality of the inflections, a not quite successful device that led him to find a hitherto unthought-of way of transmitting speech over an electrified wire. His methods were to remain basic in the teaching of the deaf.

In time, Alexander Graham Bell was to play a large part in Helen's life, at Washington, in his house facing the Potomac, or on Cape Breton island, where he lived in the summer,. and it was he who advised her father to write to the Perkins Institution and ask Michael Anagnos for a teacher for her. Anagnos too was to play his part in the drama of Helen's unfolding life, for this former Athenian journalist whom Howe had met during a visit to Greece was the first to spread her fame around the world. A shepherd boy from the hills of Epirus who had gone to the University of Athens and who had become an excellent classical scholar, he was to influence no doubt Helen's own Greek studies, for with him devotion to Greece was almost a religion. Meanwhile, as Dr. Howe's successor who had established in Boston the first kindergarten for little blind children, Anagnos was interested at once in Helen, as Dr. Bell had been, and set about finding a teacher for her. He finally chose Anne Sullivan, who had lived for six years at the Institution, as a half-blind child herself with a story behind her; and this young woman, who was fourteen years older than Helen, arrived at Tuscumbia in the spring of 1887. She brought with her as a gift from

the children at the Perkins Institution a doll that had
been dressed by Laura Bridgman. Helen, who was
standing at the door, aware of unusual goings-on,
rushed at the intruder and almost threw her down.
She felt only hostility and anger in the presence of
this stranger.

Such was the advent of "Teacher," as Helen was to
call her all through life, in a sense that had some of
the overtones of the Hindu word *guru,* as if Anne
Sullivan had been her spiritual guide; for, independent as Helen was, astonishingly so, when she grew up,
she looked upon Anne Sullivan as the builder of her
conscious being. Anne had evoked a soul from the
cipher she had been, and the process began that very
day when Teacher, with this fury in her arms, carried
her upstairs, screaming, for a first lesson. While Anne
had studied Dr. Howe's records of his work with
Laura Bridgman, she had to feel her way into a method
of her own, which Helen was to describe in time in
The Story of My Life, a tale that became a part of
American folklore. But she told Helen little of her
own story, a slice of life as harsh and sad, up to the
time of her arrival at the Perkins Institution, as anything one found in the novels of Dickens. Fourteen
years old, she had appeared sans toothbrush, coat or
hat, with a pair of clumsy boots that were much too
small and with only a chemise and some stockings
tied up in a bundle; and there she had been drawn
to Laura Bridgman, who was almost as lonely as her-

self, and had learned the manual alphabet to talk
with her. Living in the same cottage with her, she
had spelled into Laura's hand the gossip of the other
girls and the news of the day. A series of operations
more or less rectified her eyes, although she was to
be totally blind at the end of her life, while at the
moment she was illiterate and almost as unruly as
Helen was when the two were to meet in Alabama.
By what miracle in six years had she acquired the education that enabled Madame Montessori to call her
the "creator of a soul"? She might have said that it
all began with the classes in Shakespeare at the Institution which aroused in her a feeling for the magic of
both literature and learning.

It was not until many years later that Anne shared
with Helen what she called the "dark knowledge" of
her earlier life, the precocious acquaintance with human depravity that she had acquired as an orphan,
abandoned with her brother, in a Massachusetts almshouse. She had seen evil enough as a child of the Irish
"famine poor" who was placed in the women's ward
of this squalid institution, where all the twenty-
seven foundlings received that year had died and
seventy out of eighty had died the year before. She
had been surrounded from the age of ten with crazy
old bedridden women, tubercular, cancerous, per-
verted, crippled, grotesque, and with ignorant un-
married girls whose babies were covered with sores
and whose talk was all of seduction, starvation and

rape. The only playroom for herself and her brother, who was finally wheeled away himself, was the dead-house at the end of the ward where big grey rats scurried about with cockroaches during the night. Anne never forgot the clattering sound of the metal wheels of the wagon on which corpses from the ward were carried out.

There was little of the dark side of life that Helen did not know when she grew up and considered the causes of blindness,—so often the product of poverty and untalked-of diseases,—for Anne, who was down-right and realistic, freely discussed the world with her when she was old enough to assimilate this knowledge. But to keep the grim facts at a certain impersonal distance she continued to withhold the story of her own bleak childhood; and, meanwhile, she found it a "privilege to love and minister," as she wrote, "to such a rare spirit" as Helen became. Within a month the vixen, the furious little termagant, had been trans-formed into a gentle child, contentedly stringing her beads and serenely crocheting, revealing already what Anne called the beautiful intelligence that she was to spend years developing with unheard-of devotion. It was a problem to control her without breaking the spirit of this hardy, healthy, lively seven-year-old, deaf, blind and unable to utter a word, unable even to comprehend that words were related to things or that words existed. When the word "doll" was spelled into her hand, she could not make the connection at all, although she began to manipulate the claws of her old setter Belle, trying to teach the dog to spell this word. It was only when Anne held Helen's hand under the spout in the pump-house that she connected the word "water" with the cool stream, realizing for the first time that things had names and that the manual alphabet was the key to them all. Suddenly, Helen was to write, "there was a strange stir within me,—a misty consciousness, a sense of something remembered. It was as if I had come back to life after being dead . . . I understood that it was possible for me to communicate with other people by these signs. Thoughts that ran forward and backward came to me quickly,—thoughts that seemed to start in my brain and spread all over me. I think it was in the nature of a revelation. . . . I felt joyous, strong, equal to my limitations. Delicious sensations rippled through me, and sweet strange things that were locked up in my heart began to sing."

Up to this time she had felt as if invisible hands were holding her, for all her frantic efforts to escape, whereas now she had a sense of light and hope; and she was highly excited all the way back from the pump-house, learning the name of each object she explored on the path. She learned Anne's name, "Teacher," first and within a few hours she had mastered thirty words, while Anne talked into her listening fingers as one talks into a baby's ears and Helen ran, skipped and jumped to act these words

out. For one of Anne's first procedures was to teach
her how to play, how to romp, tumble, swing and
hop. The education, thus begun, continued in the
garden-house, the vine-covered cottage to which their
meals were sent, for Anne felt she must separate
Helen from the family at first, although most of the
lessons of that spring and summer were carried on
out of doors under big trees or on rambles in the
woods. Teacher and pupil followed old cow-paths
or loitered in the family burying-ground or the garden
of Andrew Jackson's abandoned dwelling, gathering
armfuls of laurels and ferns, swamp-flowers and golden-
rod or hunting for persimmons among the leaves and
weeds. They sat under a wild tulip tree where Helen,
on the warm grass, heard all about the sun, the wind,
the rain, and how the birds built their nests and the
animals found shelter, touching objects while learning their names, whether pine trees, hickories, pop-
lars, oaks, or pigs, lambs, butterflies, katydids, frogs
or crickets. She felt the fuzzy cotton-seeds, the bursting cotton-bolls, the wild-flowers close to the ground,
the dogwood blossoms, holding an egg in her hand,
for instance, and feeling the chick imprisoned within
pecking its way out into the world. She and Anne
climbed trees and sat and studied there, while the
breeze rustled through the leaves around them. In
a tree they read together *How Plants Grow*, a botani-
cal book that threw light on the development of corn
and explained why watermelons sprawled over the

ground, while Anne used all manner of means in her lessons, hooks and lines for catching fish, seed catalogues, a miniature store stocked with provisions. Everything that hummed or buzzed, sang or bloomed was a part of Helen's education, and the odour of daisies in later years brought back for her these mornings when she had learned new worlds and the names of things.

Almost every day the two walked to Keller's Landing, a tumble-down wharf on the Tennessee river, used in far-off days for landing troops in the Civil War but now overgrown with weeds and moss. There in the sunny silence teacher and pupil built dams with pebbles and made river-beds and islands, hills and lakes. It never occurred to Helen that she was learning geography when Anne constructed raised maps in sand and clay so that she could feel mountains and valleys and the windings of streams, or when she described volcanoes and glaciers, moving rivers of ice, and told her about ancient buried cities. Then a friend sent them a collection of fossils, with mollusc shells beautifully marked and sandstone bearing the prints of claws and ferns, and Helen learned of an unknown age when enormous creatures tramped over the world and died, before men appeared, in dismal swamps. Anne read to her Hans Christian Andersen's tales and some of the New England nature poets, among them Holmes and Whittier, whom she was to meet, and Helen soon learned to read herself from cardboard slips her teacher made with words printed on them in raised letters. She perceived that every word stood for a quality, object or act, she learned the difference between the words *on* and *in,* and she soon realized the meaning of abstract ideas. What did the word *think* mean? Anne told her to connect it with a certain process in her mind, the process of puzzling over her mistakes when she was doing her best to string beads of different sizes in symmetrical groups.

Helen was to write in later years that all her lessons had had in them the breath of the woods and the perfume of flowering trees, for she was especially responsive to odours, the fragrance of the mimosa and the musk-scented grapes on the arbour at the end of the garden. She was never to forget the strange odour that came up from the earth in the moments that preceded a thunder-storm. On her part, Anne was already observing certain traits of Helen that were to become more marked as time went on,—for one, the pertinacity and the love of perfection that accompanied her singleness of purpose. She was unwilling to leave a lesson if she did not understand it all, and even at the age of seven she would never drop a task until she had mastered it completely. But for this Anne herself was in part responsible, for she never praised the child unless her efforts equalled the best that normal children could achieve, and Helen later remembered her saying, "You will be glad when you recall the merciless prodding to which I subjected you." Anne was bent on teaching Helen how to protect herself against the hostile elements of nature and the world, and she always treated Helen as if she were a seeing and hearing child whom no one was ever allowed to pity. For she knew how destructive was this element of pity, along with the over-protectiveness that led to so many tragedies for the blind. As Helen wrote in later years, "A person who is severely impaired never knows his hidden sources of strength until he is treated like a normal human being and encouraged to shape his own life." She called pity "the chief stumbling block to the sightless," and she remembered that Anne had never permitted anyone to praise anything she did that was not done well. It was Anne's dream to mould a deaf-blind creature to the full life of a useful normal human being.

Many years later, Helen was to say, "Fundamentally I have always felt that I was using five senses within me, and that is why my life has been full and complete." It was from the first quite natural for her to use the words "look," "see" and "hear" as if she were seeing and hearing in the physical sense, and she felt that she owed all this to Anne, with her inventive thought, who had always wished her to live among normal people. Anne had distrusted elaborate systems of education, and she was convinced that children should come and go freely, touching real objects and combining their impressions for themselves instead of following suggestions offered by teachers. What a mistake to fill their minds with artificial associations that had to be got rid of before the child could develop from actual experiences its own ideas! "Children require guidance and sympathy far more than instruction," Anne Sullivan wrote to one of her friends. "They will educate themselves under right conditions."

In a day to come, in San Francisco, at a great public meeting, standing on the same platform with Helen and her teacher, Maria Montessori said, pointing to Anne Sullivan, "I have been called a pioneer, but there is your pioneer!" For twenty years earlier than herself, Anne also had discovered that children should be encouraged to educate themselves, that teachers should forgo the pleasure of having children depend upon them and should stimulate the self-educating instincts of the children. Both Madame Montessori and Anne had found that the so-called unruliness of children was mainly the result of mishandling at the outset of their lives and that violently insubordinate children, such as Helen had been, were the strongest and potentially the most admirable natures. Both had found that, on the whole, it was natural for children to prefer what was right and good for them, for there had been no wilful naughtiness in Madame Montessori's school and Helen was a perfect example of the Montessori child. She was never happier than when she was serving others. She even had what was

called the "Montessori face," expressing a gay and
ardent interest in overcoming obstacles and in per-
forming tasks without assistance. Like the Montessori children, she had learned to sweep, dust furniture,
wash clothes and dishes, cook and dress herself, developing at the same time her powers of initiative,
of observation, curiosity, enquiry, judgment. Hungry-
minded as she was, she had excelled especially in the
pursuit of teaching and governing herself, and in certain ways even her blindness had served her well. For
at the Montessori school the children were encouraged
to bandage their eyes to enable them to develop their
tactile sense. They learned by this method to perceive all manner of tactile differences, so that they
"saw with their hands," a Montessori phrase, and they
too, in their garden in Rome, lived and learned largely
in the open air, sowing seeds and cultivating plants.

Helen Keller and Anne Sullivan, Madame Montessori said, were "by their example," her own teachers.
She had learned from them as the pupil learns from
the master, and she was to dedicate to Helen one of her
books. But this was in a future that could never
have been dreamed of in these early days of the child
in Alabama.

II

THE PRODIGY

IN THE SPRING OF 1888, when Helen was almost
eight years old, she and her teacher went north for
a visit to Boston, for Anne Sullivan wished to present
her pupil at the Perkins Institution so that Michael
Anagnos, the director, might inspect her work. Sitting
by the window on the train, Anne pictured for Helen's
inner eye the beautiful Tennessee river and the landscape they were passing, the cotton fields, the valleys
and hills, the orchards of peaches and pear trees, the
flocks of sheep, the cattle in the meadows. She described the laughing Negroes at the stations and the
farmers at their work, swiftly tattooing her words into
the hands of the little girl beside her who was never
to lose her zest for the pageant of life.

Helen was happy at the Institution to find that
all the children were able to speak to her in her own
language, the manual alphabet brought from Spain
where it had been invented by Trappist monks who
had taken the vow of silence. There too was Laura
Bridgman, now sixty years old, the celebrated blind
deaf-mute who had been the first, as everyone knew,
to be brought into any sort of contact with the world
around her. Her education, as Helen wrote later, was

the one existing fact that "bridged the chasm between mankind and me"; but what a contrast to Helen
she was, as one could see at once and as one saw more
clearly with the passing of the years. For Laura had
never been able to cope with the world and her intellectual development had stopped with childhood.
She was sitting in her room crocheting lace, and, recognizing Anne's fingers at once, she kissed Helen kindly
but would not permit her to examine the work she
was doing. "I'm afraid your hands are not clean,"
Laura said. She added, "You must not be forward
when calling on a lady," for she was disturbed by
Helen's impulsive movements. A rigid sectarian Baptist, she exhibited still the unamiable traits that Dr.
Howe had noted long before,—she was jealous and
she liked to put others in their places. She was affec-
tionate and cheerful too, but in her presence the
buoyant Helen felt like the bad little girl of the Sunday school books. Laura seemed to her like a statue
that she had once felt in a garden, so motionless she
was and her hands were so cool, like flowers that have
grown in shady places.

Teacher and pupil thereafter spent most of their
winters in the North, returning to Alabama for a
year or a season, and for three years off and on they
stayed at the Perkins Institution, although Helen
was never a regular student there. In Boston and the
region roundabout she had her first lessons in history,
climbing the Bunker Hill monument and sailing to

Plymouth, where she touched the rock on which the Pilgrims landed. At the Institution she was soon reading *Little Lord Fauntleroy, The Arabian Nights, The Pilgrim's Progress,* Lamb's *Tales from Shakespeare,* and, already familiar with *Little Women,* she visited Concord as well and was taken through the houses of Emerson, Hawthorne and Alcott. Able to dive and swim under water, she especially liked tobogganing, swooping down through snow-drifts over a lake; and meanwhile Michael Anagnos followed her growth at the Institution, regarding her as what he called the "Eighth wonder of the world." Dr. Howe's name had attracted there all manner of celebrities, among them Oscar Wilde, long after Dickens, and the friends who gathered about the Howes,—for Julia Ward Howe had lived there too,—included most of the New England illuminati. From Whittier and Holmes to Phillips Brooks, the greatest divine in the region, with Thomas Wentworth Higginson and Dr. Hale, they were in touch with the Perkins Institution, and Helen soon became known to them all and was corresponding with them, while Michael Anagnos spread her fame abroad. He visited her family in Alabama, where he remarked that Mussel Shoals was the only spot in America that reminded him of Greece, and, returning for a visit to his own country, he read to the Queen of Greece a letter he had just received from Helen. But the queen had already heard of Helen, as Queen Victoria also had when Phillips Brooks was presented to her in London; for, with one or two others, Michael Anagnos had talked all over Europe about this "intellectual prodigy," this "marvel" in Boston. Before Helen was twelve, in fact, the details of her education were followed all over America and in Europe as well.

Anne Sullivan was distressed by this. She felt there was danger in so much publicity, and indeed the reports of Anagnos were so florid and excessive that many people disbelieved the story. A few were led to believe that Helen was a fraud, for what could one make of the legend about this "wonder girl" that spread, as the years passed, all over the world? It was said she could speak fluently, play the piano and demonstrate problems in geometry by means of her playing blocks,—myths that sprang out of Anagnos's exaggerations. Yet the facts could scarcely have been overstated, for this little girl's vigorous mind had triumphed over her disabilities, the lack of the two faculties, hearing and sight, that had always been regarded as indispensable even for common achievements. At no age at all she was deep in German, soon to be followed by Latin and Greek, and at ten, without any assistance, she wrote to Anagnos, who was in Greece, a long idiomatic letter in French. It was at ten that she learned to speak, using her sense of touch to catch vibrations of the throat and movements of the mouth, for she had heard that in Norway a deaf-blind child had been so taught and she felt that whatever had been done she could do as well. It was true,

she was never to speak very clearly and her voice
remained the great disappointment of her life. Asked,
at twelve, what book she would like to take on a long
railroad journey, she replied, "Paradise Lost," which
she read on the train; and at thirteen, busy translating Latin, she tried to master French pronunciation.
At the time she was reading *Wilhelm Tell*, Racine
and La Fontaine and chuckling at the comic situa-
tions of Molière's *Le Médecin Malgré Lui*, as her
fingers moved slowly over the raised-print lines. Anne
Sullivan said that she poured out the story, dwelling
with gusto on its humour and wit, with "an active
and intense joy in life," a never-ending freshness and
eagerness of interest. Oliver Wendell Holmes was
surprised by her mastery of English.

She was not merely receptive, moreover. She was
intellectually active as well, and she had demurred
when her teacher at home said that she was too young
to understand what her father and his friends were
talking about at table. She had been ten at the time,—
the subject was the tariff,—and Helen's reply was,
"How do you know I cannot understand? I have a
good mind! And you must remember, dear Teacher,
that Greek parents used to allow their children to
listen to the conversation of those who talked wisely.
And I think they understood some of what they
heard." Anne had told Helen the Greek myths and
suggested ways in which the two could impersonate
the characters in them, making up games in which

they played Perseus and Andromeda, the Argonauts or Proserpine and Pluto. (They also played Boadicea and her Roman captors.) Then Helen had read Charles Kingsley's *Greek Heroes,* tales of the gods and the goddesses, and she was also full of Greek history at the time, drawn to it partly perhaps because of Anagnos, who noted that Helen's memory was remarkable also. One day, talking to her about Munich, where he said there were five bridges over the Isar, she said there were only four, as he had told her himself in a letter he had written to her from Vienna; and so there were, and Helen was right in correcting him again when he spoke of the height of the cross on the dome of St. Peter's. He said it was 460 feet, but no, Helen replied at once,—it was 435, as he had written in a letter from Rome. Yet, far from being conceited or vain, Helen was simple and direct and as wholly without self-consciousness as a child could be. She had far more pleasure in the use of her mind than pride in the possession of it, to reverse G. K. Chesterton's definition of a prig; and she said she liked France best of all the "geography countries" because the French people were so gay.

No wonder she was "petted and caressed enough to spoil an angel," as Anne Sullivan said at about this time, adding that she was not spoiled because she was "so loving" and so unconscious of herself. With all the wishes in the world, she had no wants, and she was like Schweitzer who, as a boy, never desired for himself what the other village boys could not have also. At twelve, at a tea that she gave for blind children, she raised $2000; at thirteen, she saved her own pennies and collected funds for a library at her birthplace in Alabama; and meanwhile she had rescued from a home for helpless paupers a Pennsylvania boy who was blind and deaf. For weeks she thought of nothing but Tommy Stringer, and, told that a large sum would be needed to employ a teacher for him, she replied at once, "We'll raise it." Then, stating the case in the newspapers and writing to everyone she knew, she gave a party for Tommy at the Institution. Phillips Brooks appeared and spoke, with Holmes and Edward Everett Hale, and even the English painter Millais sent a contribution for which Helen thanked him in a moving letter.

In short, by the age of twelve or so, Helen was walking through obstacles that others would have found prohibitive at the height of their powers, both eager and self-disciplined as she was, high-spirited, self-assured and already revealing a mind and a will of her own. When someone had interfered with her, at home,— she was eight at the time,—and Anne asked her what she was thinking about, disturbed as she evidently was by the interference, Helen had said, "I am preparing to assert my independence," and this she had been doing in the years between. From the first Anne had noted that the more difficult was any task the more it invariably excited and interested

Helen, and she had, as everyone observed, a power of concentration that ordinary people never knew. Her disabilities drove her down to deeper levels of the will than the normal discover in themselves, and she was already reversing, moreover, some of the unhappier traits that had always been imputed to the blind. For where they were apt to have lowered vitality, hers was always higher, and she was adventurous where they were apt to be timid. But the most unusual fact about her was that, before she had entered her teens, she had discovered in herself the philosophic mind. At twelve she wrote to Michael Anagnos, "Yesterday I found Athens on the map, and I thought about you"; and one day she turned to Anne suddenly and said, "Such a strange thing has happened. I have been in Athens! I have been far away all this time, and I haven't left the room." It came over her instantly what this meant, that her mind had a reality independent of all conditions of place or body,—how else could she have been so vividly present in a place that she had never seen, so far away? It was evident, then, that space meant nothing to spirit. Later Helen Keller wrote, "The fact that my little soul could reach out over continents and seas to Greece, despite a blind, deaf and stumbling body, sent another exulting emotion rushing over me. I had broken through my limitations and found in touch an eye . . . Deafness and blindness, then, were of

no real account. They were to be relegated to the
outer circle of my life."

In time, in college, she was to find her "absolute"
in the phrase of Descartes,—which expressed this
experience,—"I think, therefore I am"; and she had
risen up actively on her "little island of limitations,"
having found a way to "bridge over the dark silent
void." For this enabled her to feel that since deafness
and blindness were not part of her mind they were
not an essential part of her existence; and an intuitive feeling of this gave her, even as a child, the
freedom and the objectivity that so surprised others.
No wonder that for Anagnos her story was "as fascinating as a fairy-tale," while almost every magazine
one picked up during these years referred, in some
way, to her achievements. Anne noted that she appealed to the sense of wonder in people's minds,
while she feared herself the ill effects this notoriety
might have on the "bright and lovely child" who
was in her care. "I know she is destined to be the
instrument of great good in the world," Anne wrote
in one of her letters, "showing how much can be
achieved under the worst difficulties and how sweet
life can be under the darkest cloud."

Anne went on to say, "There is something about
her that attracts everyone . . . her joyous interest
in everybody and everything"; and, while Phillips
Brooks wrote her long letters from Europe, she was

visiting Whittier on the Merrimac River and Oliver Wendell Holmes in his Beacon Street study. Whittier had a collection of his poems in raised print, and Helen read aloud *In School Days* to him. Dr. Holmes invited her to call one Sunday in early spring, and, seeing him often afterwards, she recited to him *The Chambered Nautilus,* a poem that for others symbolized the growth of her own mind. Edward Everett Hale sent shells from Spain to his "little cousin," and the still youthful William James visited her at the Institution, bringing with him a beautiful ostrich feather. "I thought you would like the feather," he said. "It is soft, light and caressing." Then Alexander Graham Bell, intensely interested in her education, took her first to the Washington zoo and with her teacher, presently, to the World's Fair in Chicago in 1893. Alive with curiosity, as Helen was, from top to toe, the fair for her was an Arabian Nights in real life, and, permitted to touch the objects, she did so as eagerly as Pizarro seized,—so she later put it,—the treasures of Peru. Seeing more with her fingers, as people said, than they saw with their eyes, she lived for a moment in India with its animal gods, in the land of the pyramids with its mosques and canals, riding on a camel's back, in the lagoons of Venice and even in Japan. Professor Morse of Salem, who had lived in Japan for many years, showed her the Japanese exhibit of bronzes and prints, musical instruments, books and sculptures in stone, inviting her to visit his Peabody Museum. She went up on the Ferris wheel, she explored the Viking ship, she felt the relics of the Aztecs in the Mexican exhibit, touching machinery in motion as well and learning about the process of mining diamonds in the Cape of Good Hope exhibit. With Dr. Bell talking into her hands, she soon knew much about all these countries that she was to visit herself in later life.

More than anyone else, during these years, it was Alexander Graham Bell who gave Helen her first conception of the progress of mankind, telling her as much about science as Phillips Brooks told her about religion, beginning with the story of Darwin and his *Origin of Species*. Then he told her heroic tales like those that thrilled her in the epics of Greece,—for one, the story of the laying of the Atlantic cable far, far down under the ocean. She grieved over the lives that were lost in that vast undertaking, while it excited her to think of human words fluttering along wires down there in the dark. Several times in Washington she and Anne visited Dr. Bell, sitting on his piazza overlooking the river, discussing phonetics with him while the boats passed by. They drove out in the country with him in the springtime, gathering wild azalea, honeysuckle and dogwood blossoms. Then, as they waited one day for a street-car, he placed her hand on a telephone pole and asked her what the vibrations meant to her, saying that, humming as they were all day and all night, the telephone wires were singing the story of life. They were carrying the news of birth and death, war and finance, failure and success from station to station around the world. On another day, while they were waiting in the rain, Bell placed her hand on the trunk of an oak and she felt the silvery murmur of the leaves above her. They were telling one another a lot of little things, she thought, and for years after that she liked to touch trees in the rain. Dr. Bell gave her a cockatoo called Jonquil because of its yellow crest. It perched on her foot as she read, rocking back and forth. Then it would hop on her shoulder, rub its head against her face and place its long hooked bill beside her mouth.

Dr. Bell took her also to Niagara Falls, where she felt the tremendous vibrations of the rush of water by placing her hand on the window of the hotel near by. Then she returned with her teacher to New York, where she was to spend two years at a school for the deaf. She climbed the Statue of Liberty there, and there she met first or last the men who were leaders in American literature and art. She met Andrew Carnegie too, John D. Rockefeller, Woodrow Wilson and Joseph Jefferson, the old Rip van Winkle of the stage. Ellen Terry and Sir Henry Irving assumed their favourite roles for her, while she breathlessly followed their changes of expression and their gestures, and Joseph Jefferson acted for her two

of his most famous parts, Rip and Bob Acres in *The
Rivals.* Feeling his movements with her hands, she
caught all his drolleries, as the courage of poor Bob
oozed out at the prospect of the duel; then Jefferson
gave his coat a hitch and his mouth a twitch and suddenly Bob had turned into Rip van Winkle. John
Burroughs, John LaFarge and Frank R. Stockton
were all drawn to Helen; Charles Dudley Warner
wrote an article about her, and the novelist William
Dean Howells told her about Venice where, years
before, he had been the American consul. As he
talked, with her fingers against his lips, one could
see each detail strike fire in her mind and, as someone said, throw the flash of it into her face. Two
poets, famous at the time, wrote poems about Helen
Keller,—Edmund Clarence Stedman and Richard
Watson Gilder, who told her, besides, about his moonlight journey to the pyramids of Egypt over the desert.
When Dr. Hale wrote to her, he pricked his signature in braille, and Gilder made a mark deep in the
paper to enable her to feel his signature. But, after
Alexander Graham Bell, Helen's best friend was
Mark Twain, whom she met first at a party in the
house of Laurence Hutton. At the end of two hours
someone asked her if she could remember the feeling of the hands of the company and distinguish
between them. One after another filed past and
Helen shook hands with them all, greeting in every
case the owner of the hand and uttering the name

that belonged to it without hesitation. When Mark Twain, leaving, patted her head lightly, she exclaimed, "Oh, it's Mr. Clemens."

At that time, Helen was fourteen, and Mark Twain said that whoever met her felt "a new grace in the human spirit" and "a new fragrance in the human flower." While he aroused in Helen feelings of mingled affection and awe, he called her a new marvel to wonder over in the miracle-breeding forces of humankind. When she told him she was happy he felt obliged to reply that the happy were "about as thick as white blackbirds in hell." Now and then, as she sat beside him, with her fingers listening to his talk, he would feel impelled to say something she should not hear, and he would remark, "Now, Helen, I must curse," as he removed her hand gently from his lips. He wrote to her once that, in all probability, there was nothing in heaven like their friendship or likely to be until they could show off there, and he advised her to practise with a tin halo, saying he was doing this himself. She and Anne were to see much of him as the years advanced.

When Mark Twain was carried out of himself by some deep indignation, he would suddenly rise and stand like an eagle on a crag, his plumage all ruffled by the storm of his feeling. So Helen wrote years later, and she might have been recalling his anger over the incident of *The Frost King*. This was a story that Helen had written as a birthday present for Michael Anagnos, and it was discovered that somebody else had written it first and Helen had repeated it almost word for word. How had this happened? No one knew until the old story came to light in a house where Helen had stayed long before, and it was obvious that Helen had heard the story read, after which it had buried itself in her subconscious mind. Her phenomenal power of concentration accounted for it all, and in any case there was nothing unique about it; but Michael Anagnos, up in arms over what he considered this plagiarism, set up a tribunal to study and report on the question. There were eight judges, four of them blind, in this court of investigation, "solemn donkeys," one and all, Mark Twain said, adding that he "couldn't sleep for blaspheming about it." Connecting Helen with Joan of Arc, about whom he was planning to write a book, he was incensed over this treatment of her. The gallantry of the little girl recalled to him that other child "alone and friendless in her chains, confronting her judges," and he denounced this "plagiarism farce," so "owlishly idiotic and grotesque." He called the court "a collection of decayed human turnips . . . a gang of dull and hoary pirates piously setting themselves the task of disciplining and purifying a kitten that they think they've caught filching a chop." Were they not all plagiarists themselves? Were not most ideas second-hand, consciously or unconsciously drawn from a million outside sources?

Had he not himself unconsciously stolen from Oliver Wendell Holmes the dedication for *The Innocents Abroad,* and had not Dr. Holmes told him that he, in turn, had in all probability stolen it from someone else? But there was no appeasing Michael Anagnos. For a while he blew hot and cold in regard to Helen, but in the end he broke off relations with her. He bitterly resented, for the rest, Anne Sullivan's "ingratitude" for taking Helen away from the Perkins Institution. She wished Helen to grow up freely in the outside world, whereas Helen had been his bright particular star. As Helen said, he shut them both out of his heart.

The sad affair of *The Frost King* was crucial from Helen's point of view, for it filled her with anxiety, doubt and fear. She was tortured for several years by the uncertain feeling that possibly what she wrote was not her own, that she was repeating something she had heard or read, something that was not out of her own life and mind. Meanwhile, Mark Twain interested himself in raising a fund for her education, to pay Helen's way through school and college,—for her father had died and her family was unable to do so; and, after returning to Cambridge to study, she passed without conditions the entrance examinations for Radcliffe College. By that time she was sixteen, and the headmaster of her Cambridge school said that no student he had known had ever prepared for college in so brief a time. She seemed to

regard difficulties as merely "new heights to be scaled,"
he said, and what for others were tasks were, for her,
pleasures. Yet, for her benefactors as well as herself,
the obstacles she had to surmount were many and
perplexing. She had to have expensive textbooks
copied in braille for her and other books had to
be borrowed from Germany and England,—for few
books at that time had been printed for the blind,—
and she had a typewriter equipped with movable
shuttles and a special cylinder for Greek. She had a
machine for embossing algebra and another apparatus
for constructing the geometrical figures she could
not see; while for her work in Latin prosody Anne
devised a system of signs that indicated the quanti-
ties and metres. In school and college alike, moreover,
Anne sat beside her rapidly spelling the lectures into
her hands, looking up words in dictionaries and spelling them into her hands as well and reading to her
books in philosophy, history, economics. Syllable by
syllable, she read to Helen, in languages she did not
know herself, now Mérimée's *Columba*, now Lessing's
Minna von Barnhelm, or Terence, Plautus or Heine's
travel papers, while Helen, among many other books,
read the Æneid and the Iliad herself, with as little
assistance as possible from dictionaries. By the time
she left college, after an interval, in 1904, she had a
perfect reading knowledge of Greek, Latin, German
and French, and the myth had gone abroad that Helen
Keller was "a sort of Pico della Mirandola in petti-

coats." So a French interviewer said, adding that she was "saved from pedantry by an overflowing gaiety and joy of life."

Years later Woodrow Wilson asked her why she had chosen Radcliffe in preference to Smith, Wellesley or Bryn Mawr. She answered, "Because they didn't want me at Radcliffe, and, being stubborn, I chose to override their objections." Then he asked her if a personal triumph was worth so much trouble, a question to which perhaps she did not reply, but she might have answered it by saying that her disabilities had bred a sort of over-determination. It was known that no favours were granted at Radcliffe, and she wanted to prove publicly that she was not "another American bluff," or so, at least, she said on one occasion; while she also said that she wished to demonstrate by completing her college course how far the doubly handicapped could be developed.

But what a prodigious effort it certainly required to accomplish even one-tenth of what she accomplished! Emma Goldman, in *Living My Life,* said that Helen Keller had strengthened her faith in "the almost illimitable power of the human will," and Helen had cultivated this will by welcoming impediments as well as by certain forms of auto-suggestion. She had fixed her mind, in Schiller's play, on the great figure of Joan of Arc, she liked to dwell on Columbus's perseverance, exploring a world that was almost as dark as her own, and she thought of

Socrates drinking the hemlock rather than surrender, just as she thought of Ulysses, "steadfast to the end." His too had been "the courage of a soul sore tried," as Helen wrote later, looking backward, remembering the days when, permitted to touch the casts in the Boston art museum, she had met her old friends, the deities of Homer and Virgil. She had entered the lecture-halls, she said, in the spirit of the young men who had gathered about Socrates and Plato, while in some ways she suggested Isabel Archer. For, like Henry James's heroine, she too "spent half her time in thinking of beauty, and bravery, and magnanimity. She had a fixed determination to regard the world as a place of brightness, of free expansion, of irresistible action." To her also life was worth living only if one moved in a realm of light.

III

WRENTHAM

A FEW HOURS after Helen Keller had taken her Radcliffe degree, she and Anne Sullivan set out for the village of Wrentham where, by selling some shares of stock that had been placed in their hands, they had bought a roomy old neglected farmhouse. Seven ragged acres of land surrounded the dwelling. Wrentham was twenty-six miles from Boston, and Helen knew it well. She had stayed there while she was preparing for college with the family of "The Listener," the old naturalist and journalist Joseph E. Chamberlin, who had rambled through the woods with her, telling her about the trees, the flowers and the birds. He talked about the creatures that loved shady places and hid in holes in the ground and crevices in walls, and he was the first to tell her about William Morris's *News from Nowhere* and the socialism that soon meant much to her. On Chamberlin's land, near the lake, the Indian chief King Philip was supposed to have died under a great oak tree. Helen had learned canoeing there, steering by the scent of the watergrasses and the bushes growing on the shore. She had longed to live on a farm, like her father's in Alabama, with animals, an orchard and a garden.

The house needed only a few alterations, and Helen had a study of her own, formed from two pantries and the dairy-room thrown together. Below, there was a glass door opening into a cluster of pines where she could sit by herself thinking and dreaming, and the windows were full of plants she tended, while the rooms were sunny, and a balcony opened out of her upstairs bedroom. Walking there, she could feel the vibrations of the rustling pines near by, and once when the rail shook in a fashion that was new to her she became aware that a whippoorwill stood near her, singing. It was perched on the corner post a few feet away. A bas-relief of Homer hung on the wall, so that she could feel the features of the great blind poet, the bitter traces of a mind acquainted with sorrow; and she imagined him chanting his lines of life, love and war as he groped his way from camp to camp. She felt that Greek was the loveliest language that she knew anything about,—the violin, as she called it, of human thought; and she read it until the tips of her fingers bled. She arranged her braille library in the study, with Plato and Æschylus also in Greek and with Tacitus, Catullus, Plautus and Horace in Latin. There were her favourite German books and Pascal, with others, in French. Among her English poets were Shakespeare, Pope and Dryden, Keats, Shelley and Browning. The Americans she loved best were Emerson, Thoreau and Whitman.

Up at six every morning, Helen dressed and arranged her hair, tidied her room, made beds and set the table, picking flowers for the various rooms, washing the dishes with Anne and starting the windmill running to fill the tank. Every week she pricked out the laundry list in braille, checking it a few days later when the laundry came back. At Radcliffe she had gone on ten-mile tramps with the other girls, and once on a tandem bicycle she had ridden forty miles, sleighing also on winter nights in an old haywagon and walking in the springtime in Middlesex Fells. Loving sports of every kind, she liked tobogganing in Wrentham too, and she went horseback riding with Anne, who sometimes held the reins or let the horse wander alone if he was gentle. On walks she would plunge into the underbrush, scrambling out scratched and bruised, only to insist on doing it again,—for she would never admit that she was hurt; and in general she loved speed as she loved dogs. One of these, a great Dane, upset the supper-table and knocked over another table with a lamp before Anne discovered that he was almost blind. Helen was presented with a huge mastiff that frightened everybody else and was finally shot by a policeman, and when this got into the newspapers hundreds of letters arrived from people who were eager to give her another. She had, first or last, a French bullterrier, a Lakeland terrier, a brindle Dane, a German police-dog, a Shetland collie, and Thora, who became the parent of a numerous offspring. Anne at-

tempted a little amateur farming. Helen climbed the
apple trees and shook down the apples in the fall,
but in the end they gave up tending the orchard
because the deer stripped the bark off most of the
trees.

One great question filled Helen's mind: what was
her special niche in the world? She had constantly
asked herself in college how she could use the education that had cost others so much in effort or in
money, and she felt that, if she could find it, there
must be some particular task through which she
could pay back her debt to life. At the moment there
were many people who thought they were more com-
petent than either Anne or she to decide this matter.
Carmen Sylva, the Queen of Roumania, wrote that
she had a plan for her, to manage a pleasant home
for the Roumanian blind. She wanted Helen to
work with her and she broke off their correspondence
when Helen replied that she could not do this. The
queen was convinced that Helen was selfish and
really cared nothing for the welfare of the blind,
whereas Helen, who had grown up herself outside
an institution, believed that the blind should be
helped to help themselves. She was not in sympathy
with the notion of segregating the handicapped and
felt that they should be trained to live in the world,
and she thought Carmen Sylva's plan was a senti-
mental dream, by no means according with modern
methods. As it happened, Carmen Sylva was one of

a series of queens who were to be interested in Helen, among them Queen Victoria, Queen Elizabeth of England, the Queen of Greece and Queen Wilhelmina of Holland. The Queen of Spain sent her a medallion portrait of herself.

Besides Carmen Sylva, there were others who tried to force Helen's mind, and Mark Twain backed her up when she withstood the presuming souls who were sure they knew the path she ought to follow. "I always suspect anyone," he said, "who has entered into partnership with God without his knowledge." Helen herself already felt that her work was to be for the blind but she was uncertain how to go about it, and, longing to speak like other people, she felt she would have to improve her speech before she made a practice of appearing in public. However, she joined a Boston society to promote the welfare of the blind, appealing to the legislature to appoint a commission. She was resolved, as she wrote later, that, whatever role she played in life, it was not going to be passive; but self-doubt and a sense of isolation overwhelmed her at the moment. She said it enfolded her sometimes like a cold mist as she sat alone and waited at life's shut gate. It was Walt Whitman who restored her self-confidence and courage. "When I read *The Song of the Open Road*," she was to write in *Midstream*, "my spirit leaped up to meet him." Later she was to say at a Whitman dinner, "He has opened many windows in my dark house."

Wondering, meanwhile, if her education had perhaps led to nothing, she felt that she could write or make translations, or at least emboss books for the blind, encouraged as she was by the great success of *The Story of My Life,* written and published while she was still in college. This book had been largely composed in the form of daily and fortnightly themes in a course in English composition conducted by "Copey," the well-known Mr. Copeland who had said she wrote better in some of her work than any other man or woman he had had as a pupil. Her style was imaginative, lucid, firm, precise, with images that were sometimes suggested by the Bible. Her themes had been talked about outside of college, and one of the popular magazines had paid her $3000 for the publication rights of the serial story. She had already been asked, at twelve, for a sketch of her life for a magazine, but this was an undertaking on a larger scale, and she had had the assistance of a young Harvard and Radcliffe instructor who helped her to organize the book. John Macy had learned the manual alphabet to talk with her about it, and, when the manuscript was complete in 1903, it was put into braille so that Helen could read it and correct it. Writing was physically difficult for her, whether she composed on a typewriter or placed a grooved board between the pages to enable her to keep the lines quite straight, or whether she wrote with the cumbersome braille machine with which she produced a manuscript that she could read. If she worked on the typewriter, she could not refer to the pages again unless they were read back into her hands by somebody's fingers, and she was obliged to prick notations with a hairpin on the pages in order to keep track of their sequence. But nevertheless she had written a quite long book. John Macy added a collection of her letters and an account of Anne Sullivan's work that supplemented her own story of her life and education. This book was to appear, sooner or later, in about fifty languages, among them Oriya, Cebuano, Hiligayon, Telalog, Ilocano, Kanaada, Pushtu, Telugu and Tamil.

It was not long before John Macy, who had largely shaped the book, became an important part of Helen's life, especially after 1905 when he and Anne Sullivan were married in a ceremony performed by Edward Everett Hale. Eleven years younger himself than Anne, Macy had become a journalist, but for him Boston, where he worked, had lost all its literary interest and was simply a case of life-in-death survival. At Harvard, as one of the circle of Copey, he had been drawn to William James whose liberal way of talking philosophy, with none of its Babu words, had opened all manner of lighted clearings for him. James's alertness and nonchalance had delighted Macy, along with his holiday explorations in what he once described as "the open air of human nature." He "turned poet and prophet," Macy said, "in the midst of an intellectual picnic and spoke with an eloquence which no man less than a genius" could approach. Macy himself, with a life of Poe and various essays that were light in touch, had made a name for himself as an imaginative critic, a disciple of Remy de Gourmont and one of the bright spirits of the critical movement that was harrowing the ground for the literary revival of the twenties. He always rejoiced in the rare experience of watching the dawn of a new literary light for eyes that were accustomed, as he put it, to uncertainty and darkness. Writing of Shakespeare and Dante, he relished Wells and Bernard Shaw, and Maeterlinck, "a great child playing with flowers and words," and, as literary editor of *The Nation,* a few years later, he was to greet James Joyce and D. H. Lawrence. In *The Spirit of American Literature* he produced a work that for two generations remained by far the best handbook written on the subject.

Meanwhile, joining the household at Wrentham, he was to corroborate Helen's own tastes, for he shared her feeling about William James, Walt Whitman and Mark Twain, in whom she delighted as an author as well as a friend. The first play she had witnessed was *The Prince and the Pauper,* and *Life on the Mississippi,* as she told Mark Twain himself, was her favourite story of adventure, all the more exciting to her because at Memphis, as a child, she had gone over one of the old Mississippi steamboats. She admired both William James and Whitman for the same reason that Macy admired them, because, while neither had any delusions about the intelligence of the human herd, they never lost a deep faith in its possibilities. Both agreed that Whitman was our one magnificent American poet, and Helen responded actively when Macy read Stevenson into her hand, with William James, Thoreau and *Huckleberry Finn*. She had read in college Schopenhauer, Nietzsche, Bergson, Tolstoy and Karl Marx, and Macy introduced her to Romain Rolland, Hardy, Kropotkin, Anatole France and Wells, leading her deeper every day into the world of socialism of which "The Listener" had told her during her school years. At Radcliffe, with the other girls, popping corn on winter nights and drinking cider before the blazing hearth, she had discussed the altruistic movements of the time, the rising tide of the masses and the brotherhood of peoples. Her mind had been full of the panaceas that were going to bring paradise on earth and replace with perfect democracies the existing empires, and Macy convinced her that the genius of the world was permeated with socialist thought and feeling. An unbroken succession of painters, poets and men of science had been socialists, William Morris, Alfred Russel Wallace, William Dean Howells, Wells and Shaw, while with the younger writers, John Macy said, socialism was "as much the fashion as a flowing tie." There were almost enough of these to justify Lassalle's boast that "the culture of the world belongs to socialism."

So John Macy presently wrote in *Socialism in America,* adding, "We have no kings, but America is the sport of capital. It lies abjectly prostrate before a power-drunk bourgeoisie"; and all these quite obvious truths passed into Helen's mind, which was predisposed already to receive them. With Anne she had visited the squalid streets where the underdogs of society lived, the hideous sunless tenements where children grew up, half-clad and under-fed, and it outraged her that so many were condemned to a hopeless struggle for existence, a life that was a series of scrimmages, miseries, frustrations. She was aware of the social evils that were often the causes of blindness,—caused themselves so often by poverty and filth,—and she was convinced that the dominant parties were managed by the ruling class for its own privilege and profit. Economics at college, she felt, had been admirably put, but she could never harmonize this teaching with the economic facts she had learned in life; and when she read Wells's *New Worlds for Old* she was sure that John Macy was right, although Anne at first agreed with neither of them. Helen felt that the struggle of the workers resembled her own in many ways and she wished them to be helped as generously as she had been, "impassioned reformer" that she was "by temperament," in the

phrase of Anne, and destined to become still more
so as the years advanced.

Helen was grateful to Macy, for he kept her in
touch with the new tendencies in literature and the
discoveries of science, along with the more important
events of the day. He sometimes sat up all night copying her manuscripts for her, criticizing her work, at
the same time, severely, and he brought Arthur Ryder,
the Sanskrit scholar, to Wrentham too, and Walter
Conrad Arensburg, the art-collector of the future.
Helen never forgot the good conversation she shared
during these Wrentham years, when some one of the
circle was always presenting a book worth discussing
or a fresh idea or repeating fine new poetry with
felicitous effect. At one time the whole household
was brightened for a week by a reading of Synge's
Riders to the Sea and *The Well of the Saints*; and
Helen remembered later how hungry Anne was for
adventure and fun and how she delighted in the
company of intelligent people. Full as Anne was of
caprices and whims, with her buoyancy and gusto,
she liked the vivid as much as she hated the dull, the
boring women who inflicted on her their witless little
dramas, their social inanities and their incessant
chatter. She forced herself to be kind to them and
she could charm the dullest into a new appreciation
of beauty or justice, but to her they were insipid, like
the immature girls at the Perkins Institution after the
disreputable girls of the Tewksbury almshouse. Petu-

lant and humorous, unmanageable often, she disliked
prigs and the goody-good, who lacked all spontaneity
in their conscious virtue, while with her wit, her crav-
ing for beauty and her passion for excellence in every
form, she loved excitement and novelty in scenes and
people. Her moods were always changing, and, overcome by melancholy, she would sometimes disappear
for a morning or a day. She would hide in the woods
or under a boat on the lakeside; then she would re-
appear all smiling, her gay, wholesome, teasing self
again.

So, many years later, after her death, Helen was to
write about this dedicated teacher whose unwavering
devotion had imparted to her own life comeliness
and form, toiling away for years unpaid, half-blind,
poor, solitary always in her ideals and thought. There
were less than ten people in the United States, a certain authority reckoned, who had the requisite intelligence, patience and skill to teach the deaf-blind as
Anne had done, while she herself had invented
methods for the rest; and Helen remembered how full
of zest Anne's life had been until, with the wreck
of her marriage, it fell in ruins. Their days at Wrentham had been crowded with interests and pleasures.
Sometimes in the evening Helen had played solitaire,
with cards that were marked in braille in a right-hand
corner, or she did embroidery work or knitted; but
often with Macy or Anne she played checkers or chess
on a board that had been constructed for her. Squares

were cut out so that the men stood in them firmly, and the jar made by shifting the men from one square to another told her when it was her turn to play. The white chessmen were larger than the black, so that she could distinguish her opponent's manœuvres, and the white checkers were curved on top while the black were flat. It was Macy, meanwhile, who stretched the wire from tree to tree across the field so that Helen could run freely along it without hurting herself, scampering about in the rain, the snow or the wind, for she could not walk slowly and she tired Anne so much that it was Macy who joined her on most of her walks. Along the wire, on sunny days, before going back to work, Helen found her way to the woods where she could wander freely. Once in the spring all three were rebuilding old walls together, and this suggested to Helen a long poem, *The Song of the Stone Wall,* about the Yankee builders who had been her forbears. She felt the beauty of the old stones in their shapes and textures, flat, grooved, with rents and jagged edges, crumbled by the heat, polished by the cold, and Anne described to her the effects of light and shadow and the tapestry of flowers and bushes that half covered their surface. Then Macy took her to the cemetery where she could feel the moss-grown gravestones, and, reading old New England chronicles, she thought of the Puritan settlers who had forced back the wilderness inch by inch. How much New England history there was in these weather-beaten oracles of stone beside which she had walked with "searching feet," plunging and stumbling over them, following the windings of the wall down by the meadow brook and over the hill.

In this literary household John Macy and Helen were both hard at work, and there, within a few years, Helen had written *The World I Live In* and the essays that she collected in *Out of the Dark.* The poet Richard Watson Gilder, the editor of *The Century Magazine,* had urged her to explain how she received her impressions in order to answer the complaints of readers of *The Story of My Life* that she could not know what she was talking about. But long before this, in her final year at Radcliffe, she had written a little book called *Optimism,* expressing what she called a "happy disposition" that, as she said, "turns everything to good." She was in no danger of falling into the optimism that Macy attacked, the shallow Pollyanna variety that prevailed at the moment and filled so many fatuous American minds, although she had reasons, if she had indulged them, for "turning hell's back yard into a playground," in the characteristic phrase of her friend Mark Twain. She never had to handle money, she did not have to cross streets alone, she had always been able to count on personal kindness, and she had been spared the pain of many sights and sounds that afflicted those who heard and saw too much. For others blessings of this kind produced a rosy view of life, but not for the

tough-minded and humorous Helen, one of whose
mottoes was "True faith abhors preaching" and who
was always ready to laugh at herself. How she laughed,
for instance, when she had spoken too solemnly and
Anne called her an "incorrigible little sermonizer"!
One teacher with whom she read Shakespeare at school
had said that what she enjoyed best were the light
and amusing touches in *As You Like It,* along with
the serious passages in *King Henry V*; and now in
the realistic air of John and Anne Sullivan Macy
there was little chance for fatuity to lodge in her
mind. Her Emersonian *Optimism* was an honest expression of a life that was "one long battle against
obstacles," as Helen said frankly, in the world of
the deaf-blind with its "inhuman silence," which is
"not the stillness that soothes the weary senses." The
silence of the deaf blind, she continued, "severs and
estranges," for it is "never broken by a word of gaiety,
or the song of a bird, or the sigh of a breeze."

How then could Helen have been optimistic, truly
and honestly so, as she convinced her readers in this
youthful essay? The reason lay in her early discovery,
even as a little girl, of the meaning of Descartes'
"I think, therefore I am." When she had exclaimed
to Anne Sullivan, "I have been in Athens," implying
that her imagination had placed her there, she had perceived that her real life was independent of time and
place and above all independent of her own physical
being. Studying philosophy, she had overridden her

disabilities, passing through imagination into a "light-flooded resonant universe" that led her almost to forget her deafness and blindness. So she wrote later in *Midstream,* referring to these early days when she had entered so naturally the world of Spinoza and other great philosophers and poets. She understood how it was possible for Spinoza to find happiness when he was excommunicated, despised and poor, and why it meant so little to this great soul that he was suspected alike by Jew and Christian. Not that she had ever been treated so but that Spinoza's isolation from so many of the pleasures of the world was analogous to hers. She had found she could overleap space and time, crowd years of remembrance into an hour or lengthen into eternity a single minute, and she saw her true self as "a free spirit throwing to the winds" what she called "the bonds of body and condition and matter."

It was in the joy of these new thoughts that she had written *Optimism* and, following this, *The World I Live In*; and as long as she lived she was to see the importance of philosophy as "a star in lonely hours and dark passages" of life. She had taken to it intuitively, finding in Plato's ideal world a special meaning for those who were handicapped as she was, for it showed that the things you see and hear are not the true realities but imperfect manifestations of ideas. "Philosophy," she wrote, "is the history of a deaf-blind person writ large," recording the efforts of the mind to be free of the clogging material world and fly forth into the world of idea and essence. She liked to think of John Richard Green drilling himself in adversity, "shutting out the gloomy" and "calling in the bright," though she knew that the only optimism worthy of respect represented some sort of conquest over evil and sorrow. There was a dangerous optimism of ignorance and indifference, she said, and this optimism invited disaster by ignoring evil and making people negligent and heedless. She had no use for the optimism of mere good nature. But who could deny that, if she was happy, with all her deprivations, her testimony to the goodness of life deserved a hearing? Pessimism, she said, "kills the instinct that urges men to struggle against poverty, ignorance and crime and dries up all the fountains of joy in the world." That it "robs men of the incentive to fight with circumstance" she knew from her own experience of the opposite feeling, and she added, "Doubt and mistrust are the panic of a timid imagination which the steadfast heart will conquer and the large mind transcend."

As *The World I Live In* and *Out of the Dark* continued to proclaim her faith that "life is either a daring adventure or nothing,"—and as she carried out this faith in action,—the more perceptive people were the more they saw in this deaf-blind girl what Gandhi described as *satyagraha,* "soul force." In time this made Helen Keller one of the great spirits of the world, as simply and manifestly great as the grass is

green, and the larger the natures of others were the
more they were convinced of this, as Mark Twain
and Alexander Graham Bell had been convinced in
the beginning.

*   *   *

When someone remarked that Helen's concept of
things beyond the reach of her hands must lack
reality, Mark Twain's answer was, "But a well put
together *unreality* is pretty hard to beat"; and when
"Mr. Dooley" Dunne said that her life must be dull
and monotonous, his answer was, "You're damned
wrong there . . . Blindness is an exciting business,"
Mark Twain went on. "If you don't believe it, get
up some dark night on the wrong side of your bed
when the house is on fire and try to find the door."
All these years Mark Twain had woven about her
dark walls, she said, a romance and adventure that
made her feel "happy and important"; and, while
he was not a socialist, he abhorred plutocracy, though
his personal relations played havoc with his feelings
about it. Helen and Anne spent three days at Storm-
field with him before he died, and Helen was all the
happier with him because he fully realized the originality and largeness of Anne's character and work.
He was a cynic, he liked to say, but there was nothing
cynical in his hatred of cruelty, unkindness, preten-
tiousness and meanness, and Helen was drawn to
him also because his talk was "fragrant with tobacco
and flamboyant with profanity," as she put it. He

did not temper his conversation to any femininity, and he said that in her bathroom she would find Scotch whiskey and cigars or, if she happened to prefer it, Bourbon. A card in the bedroom hanging from a candlestick explained to prospective burglars where articles of value were to be found, while, referring to her own blindness, he said, "Helen, the world is full of vacant, staring, soulless, unseeing eyes." On their last evening, by the fire, he read aloud *Eve's Diary,* with Helen's fingers resting on his lips.

A few years earlier than this she had gone to Nova Scotia to visit Alexander Graham Bell at Beinn Bhreagh, the summer house at Baddeck to which he retired when he was at work on theories or inventions. He was immersed at this time in the study of aeronautics, experimenting with heavier-than-air flying-machines, and Helen flew on the windy hillside one of Dr. Bell's great kites and was almost blown out to sea as she clung to the cable. The astronomer Simon Newcomb and Professor Langley were also there, and they all went out together for a sail one day, discussing aeronautics while Helen had a lesson managing the sheets of the boat and controlling the ropes. Not treating her as a "pitiable ghost groping its way through the world," she said, Dr. Bell assumed she could understand the principle of magnetism and the laws of physics, able as he was himself to explain the most difficult problems with an irresistible vividness, energy and grace. Helen felt something large and harmonious alike in his gestures and in his thoughts. She spent a night with his two daughters in their houseboat on the Bras d'Or lake, climbing down a rope ladder into the water and swimming in the moonlight.

More than once, at this time of her life, Helen attended with Dr. Bell conventions to further the teaching of speech to the deaf, and he never tired of reciting to her, spelling into her hands, passages from *In Memoriam, Julius Caesar* and *The Tempest.* He told her there were unique tasks waiting for her, a unique woman, and one day he said to her that, if the occasion should ever arise, she should not hesitate to marry. Heredity was not involved in her case, he said, but she replied that she felt a man and a woman should be equally equipped in order to weather successfully the vicissitudes of life. For a man to marry her would be like marrying a statue. When, later, the occasion occurred, did she remember this conversation? She had felt that love was a beautiful flower but not for her to touch, though its fragrance made the garden a place of delight.

IV

OUT OF THE DARK

O NE DAY in the winter of 1912, the wife of Maurice Maeterlinck, the actress Georgette Leblanc, appeared at Wrentham, bringing love and greetings from the author of *Pelléas and Mélisande* "to the girl," as he wrote, who had "found the Blue Bird." In part because Helen was lovely to look at, she charmed the minds of artists and poets, and Maeterlinck was only one of many for whom she was the *Belle au Bois Dormant,* the sleeping beauty who had once been imprisoned in the castle. To others she suggested Ariel, confined in a cloven tree till Prospero "made gape" the pine and let him out; while for Georgette Leblanc she was a "daring little Amazon" who "struck back boldly at life" when it assailed her. This girl "assuredly is not one of the meek," Georgette Leblanc said to herself, as she drove away that sunny February morning. Helen had recited to her several passages from Maeterlinck, and she gave his wife a book for the poet inscribed with a line of his: "All stones are alike, all stones are precious, but man sees only a few of them."

Helen was erect and well-developed, Georgette Leblanc said, with a finely shaped head and well-cut regular features, with a nose almost classically straight, a full mouth nobly curved and chestnut hair drawn back into a knot behind. Encircling her brow was a black velvet ribbon, its edging prettily worked with beads, while one felt in her an impetuous force, a powerful vitality, expressed in the nervous vigour of all her movements. She was both healthy and ardent, this witness remembered, with obvious captive passions that had knocked impatiently at closed doors and then escaped by unexpected outlets. How she must have battered herself against her prison walls! With what rebellious or mad despair she must have flung herself against these doors that would not let her out! Yet her features retained no trace of the terrible battles that must have been waged within her at the awakening of life, while joyous convulsions of her whole body took one by surprise as a sudden flash of thought broke through her darkness. She started as if she had received an electric shock. Georgette Leblanc also noted her unwearying curiosity, her manner of expressing herself in images and symbols and her remark, "What woman has not longed for love? But I think it is forbidden me, like music and light." Helen added, "Happiness is like the mountain summit. It is sometimes hidden by clouds, but we know it is there."

That Helen Keller lived far more richly and far more alertly than others a Boston witness observed about this time when Dr. Richard Cabot saw her on a platform, surrounded by a company of distinguished persons. Their decorous and contented faces were lifeless, he said, in comparison with hers, and he was almost afraid they might venture too near her and "burn themselves out at the flame of her magnificent life." Her verve showed Dr. Cabot how careless and wasteful were ordinary folk,—her "net income of valuable sensations" exceeded that of others, apart from her resources of imagination and thought; and all this explained why she was beset by psychologists, neurologists, physicians, who were eager to understand the operations of her mind. She was so constantly investigated that she might have been living in a goldfish bowl,—examined as if she were an aerolite, a sunspot or an atom,—and she felt that only a merciful providence had saved her from being separated, actually separated, into electrons and ions. For her "scientific tormentors," as she called them, brought with them all manner of instruments with appalling ingenuity, strange shapes and long Greek names, instruments that pinched or pricked, squeezed, pressed, stung, buzzed or moved her fingers rapidly up and down. One of them counted her breaths, another her pulse, one ascertained whether she was hot or cold, how fear and anger tasted and whether she blushed, how it felt to swing round and round like a wooden top and what happened when rubber cuffs were inflated on her wrists. She underwent vibratory tests with tuning forks and cymbals and her head was screwed up in a vise, while Helen submitted to the inquisition hoping that something might result that would be of use to others who were deaf and blind.

The men of science knew she was not the so much talked of wonder girl who was able to make all sorts of uncanny predictions and who had never once been discouraged or sad; but, for all that, she surprised them enough, as one of them reported after a morning's drive he took with her. He asked her what she could say about the country they drove through,— of which he himself told her nothing,—and she said they were passing through open fields, then they were passing trees and finally passing a house with a fire of logs. Soon she said they were passing a group of large buildings,—a mental hospital this turned out to be,—and then a large publishing plant, which she recognized at once because her nostrils detected the ink from the presses. The doctor noted that her sensory equipment, astounding as it seemed, was due to concentration of attention. The destruction of two of her senses created a sort of emergency that led her to draw on resources which others ignore.

There was one question especially which the scientists were always curious about, the nature and the development of her dreams, supposing that these would reveal a world that was colourless, formless and flat, a vast solitude of soundless space, without perspective. She was able to say that, for one thing, in sleep she seldom groped and that she had no need of any guide. Even in· a crowded street she was self-sufficient, and in general in her dreams she enjoyed an independence that was quite foreign to her actual physical life. In dreams, moreover, she had sensations of odours and tastes, and even ideas, that she did not remember having in her conscious hours, while she relived in dreams the agonizing scenes of the Sepoy Rebellion, the French Revolution and the massacres of Jews in Russia. Cities burned before her eyes, she fought the flames until she fell, and once in her arms she held a child whom she implored the soldiers not to kill. A recurring dream was of a spirit that seemed to pass before her face emitting a blast of heat like the heat of an engine, a spirit that she felt as the embodiment of evil, remembered unconsciously perhaps from a day when she had gone too near the fire. (It was in her childhood and her clothes were in a blaze before her old nurse was able to roll her in a blanket.) Another spirit in a dream brought with it a sensation of damp and cold like that of a November night when the window is open, and this spirit, visiting her, stopped just beyond her reach, swaying back and forth like a creature in grief. She felt her blood freezing in her veins, she tried to move and cry out, and, convinced that this was death, she said to herself, "I wonder if it has taken her," meaning Anne.

It was to answer all these enquiries that Helen had published in 1908 the little book entitled *The World*

I Live In, a world she described as very largely built of touch-sensations, with less important sensations of smell and taste. There, and in *Out of the Dark,* she wrote at length about the hand, the organ of apprehension that played for her the part that hearing and sight played for others and that enabled her to read, as if she were clairvoyant, the faces and hands of people whom she met. She could distinguish the Yankee twang and the Southern drawl she had never heard by touching two or three spots on the throats of the speakers, while hands for her were as easy to recognize as faces and revealed the secrets of the character more openly, in fact. She had met a bishop with a jovial hand, a humorist with a hand of lead, a braggart with a hand that was obviously timid, a quiet apologetic man who had a fist of iron and others whose hands suggested "dormouse valour." She remembered handshakes that made one think of sudden death,—ill-boding hands, as she described them,—and in hands of a soft smooth roundness, especially of the rich who had never known toil, she felt a certain chaos of the undeveloped. Then there were those who held out civil finger-tips, retreating even as you touched them. Helen well remembered the large hands of Phillips Brooks, which she called brimful of tenderness and a strong man's joy, and Mark Twain's hands, full of drolleries and whimsies that changed to sympathy and championship while you held them.

Living in darkness and silence, Helen could feel

with her own hands the beautiful, the strong, the weak, the comic, and it was the hand that bound her to the world of others. How much of history the word "hand" embodied she liked to discuss in her books, the hand that spins and weaves, ploughs and reaps, converts clay into walls and builds roofs of the trees of the forest, the hand one finds in the Latin form of words like manual and manufacture, management, manœuvre, manumit, manacle and so on. In the Bible everything is done by the hand of the Lord or of Moses, the hand that is used in the great moments of blessing, cursing, smiting, marrying, destroying, building temples or altars and shaping the earth. Helen liked to think of the millions of people who entrusted their lives every day to the hand that grasped the throttle of a locomotive. The meanings of the word hand, she said, filled eight pages in her dictionary, and no wonder for, if one studied the hand, the more one discovered in it the true picture of man and the story of human growth.

So much for the "seeing hand" that served as eyes and ears for her and that enabled her sometimes not only to recognize her friends but even to know whether they were sad or happy. Touching flowers, she would say, "What lovely white lilacs!" feeling the difference in their texture from the lilacs that are purple, and she could tell white from red roses and white from purple pansies because in both cases the white petals are thinner than the coloured. Meanwhile, as she

wrote once, "Every atom in my body is a vibroscope"
and she could feel sounds alike through her hands
and her feet. She could feel the music-waves along
the floor when an orchestra played, so that she was
able to dance in perfect time,—she did so with blind
soldiers in hospitals after the second world war; and,
although she occasionally confused the singing voice
with the violin, she could tell when one or more instruments were playing. Listening to radio concerts,
with her fingers lightly on the board, she distinguished
the music of the oboe, the piano, the harp and the
blending of all in a chorus of triumphal vibrations.
By listening intently she recognized at least one of
Beethoven's symphonics, although, as she said, she
could never be sure of the others; and the vibrations
of a great organ in a church beat against her like
waves against a ship at sea. Only jazz disturbed her.
It was not pleasant to her touch, and it filled her,
she said in an interview once, with an impulse to flee
from a sinister presence that was about to spring
upon her. She felt it awakened shadow memories,
figures of the jungle, the cry of dumb souls that were
not yet able to speak.

For the rest, by grasping the bars of cages in a zoo
she could distinguish the voices of the animals within,
telling the tigers from the panthers and the foxes
from the wolves; and she could perceive the murmur-
ing of waters, the flutter of a bird's wing after a bath,
the movement of leaves near by and the humming of

bees. She noted the whinneying of horses and the
barking of dogs, and she could feel people's characters
in the vibrations of their footsteps. Sitting in a hotel
dining-room and following vibrations on the floor, she
perceived the various moods of those who passed her,
their firmness, indecision, fatigue, anger or sorrow,
and whether they were active, careless, deliberate or
hasty. She recognized a carpenter's hammering by
the ringing concussion of blow upon blow and his
sawing by its slanting, up-and-down toothed vibration.

But it was not merely the tactile sense that enabled
her to create a world "alive, ruddy and satisfying,"
as she somewhere called it, for her sense of taste was
active too and especially the sense of smell that she
described once as a "fallen angel." Her face would
light up as she entered a greenhouse, uttering the
names of most of the flowers, perceiving each by its
perfume and sometimes by touch. Once she exclaimed,
"A parrot plant!", astonishing the owner, who had
not known himself what this plant was. But plants
emitted other odours that were perceptible to her,
odours of the wood, as in sandalwood and cedar, or
of the bark, as in cinnamon, or of the seeds, perhaps,
or the leaves or the roots. For her the sense of smell
was the most important aesthetic sense, and it amused
her to note the meaning that Balzac attached to the
odours which came to him while he worked in his
attic in Paris. To her the odour peculiar to Paris
when she was there in later years was a blend of per-

fume, powder, wine and tobacco, and she delighted in the exhalations that reached her in city streets from automobiles, fruit-stands, drays and horses. It was because of these exhalations that she loved subways and busses that brought her into relation with the "mutable many," who were by no means "rank-scented" to her with her love of the impressions that also brought her in contact with other people. Detecting freshness and good taste in the odours of soap, silks and gloves, she could tell the work that others were engaged in by the odours of an office or of paint that clung to their clothes. She liked these intimate revelations of her fellow-creatures.

This sense made Helen Keller feel akin to the western Indians, who scented invisible camp-fires at a great distance, and she was to relate in after years how, travelling across the country, she always knew when the train was approaching oil-wells. She could smell St. Louis and Duluth from their breweries miles away, and she knew when the train was to pass Peoria long before it reached the city by the fumes of the whiskey stills that woke her up at night. Walking past churches, she always knew whether they were Catholic or Protestant and she recognized at once the Italian quarter of a town by the odour of salami and garlic. She could usually tell by odours alone what part of a city she was in, and, saying that there are "as many smells as there are philosophies," she said that Fifth Avenue was a "very odorous street."

She received olfactory impressions there of expensive perfumes, powders and creams, choice flowers and delicate foods exhaling from the houses, and, when a door was open, she knew what cosmetics were used within and whether they roasted their coffee and whether they used candles. She could tell if the house had been freshly decorated, and whether the family burned soft coal or wood, just as in London later she perceived the odours of fresh bread and of wineshops and passing motor-busses. She always knew at once when she was entering one of the parks by the aroma of the grass or the burning leaves.

Once, during these later years, she wrote an article, *Three Days to See,* saying how she would have spent these days if they had been granted her, if she had had eyes to use like other people. She would have spent the first day looking at the faces of her friends and studying the colours of rugs, pictures and books, looking too at a baby's face in order to see what preceded a sense of the conflicts that life develops. Then she would have taken a walk in the woods and noted in the evening the reality of artificial light. On the second day, she would have seen the dawn, then two museums, a natural history museum and an art museum, where she would have been able to compare the great Italian painters with the feverish vision of the moderns. In the evening she would have gone to the movies or the theatre for a glimpse perhaps of

Pavlova, Hamlet or Falstaff. On the third day she would have seen New York from the Empire State Building and the East River Bridge, making later in the day the rounds of the city. She wished to answer the question, How would you use your eyes if you had just three more days to see?

The idea had been suggested to her by the remark of a friend that she had seen "nothing in particular" while out for a walk, and Helen Keller would have liked to establish a compulsory course in colleges entitled "How to use your eyes." That her "well put together unreality" was pretty hard to beat, Mark Twain had said long before, saying too what others said,—what had become a commonplace,—that she saw more in her blindness than others who had eyes. It was true, as she herself observed, that, without imagination, her world might very well have been poor indeed, while, having it, she had been able to build, without hammer, saw or any tool, a sort of Solomon's temple in her mind. This faculty had laid the stones one upon another, creating in her what a French writer called a "second Galatea" and one who posed fundamental questions. For, in her presence, this writer asked himself what was the limit of human perfection and how far could the will overcome hostile nature. As he said, "One's imagination goes back to the creation, described in Genesis, where everything was formed out of nothing,—*omnia ex nihilo* . . . There is no limit set to our perfectibility, since from such a human zero such a sum of knowledge, emotion and vitality has been made."

No wonder Helen Keller herself believed that men are plastic and felt that their capabilities are still unknown. "We may challenge thinkers," she wrote, "to sound the resources of human nature and show what initiatives may issue from it in coming ages."

V

THE OPEN ROAD

LIKE MANY YOUNG PEOPLE of her time, Helen Keller had been impressed by Carlyle's nineteenth century gospel of work, and, "longing to accomplish," as she wrote, "a great and noble task," she was determined first to earn her own living. There were, in any case, no family funds for her, and she could not count on the rich friends who had sent her through college, for, generous and kind as they often were, they were apt to be capricious and sometimes withdrew their assistance at a critical moment. They left her all but entirely stranded when Anne Sullivan was married, as if John Macy alone could support the household, and Helen, proud and self-reliant, bent on making her own way, was apprehensive for her teacher's future. For John Mary was drifting away, and Anne, who was not robust, was threatened with a recurrence of her own early blindness. Besides, they were both open-handed and constantly contributing whatever they could spare to this cause or that, to the cause of the deaf in one country, of the blind in another, or perhaps to the strikers in New Jersey. When Helen won an award of $5000 from a magazine she turned it over to one of the foundations for the blind. It irked her that she could not respond to more of the causes she cared for, that she had to ignore appeals from all over the world.

For her own security she cared not at all, but she cared deeply for the security of Anne, who had created her, as she once put it, "out of a clod in the dark silence." Anne had "submerged herself like a stream underground," and it frightened Helen to think what would happen if she died and her teacher was left unprotected. And how could she support them both by writing? Keeping up her study of languages for its possible use in translating, she had learned Italian in addition to German and French; but this was a poor sort of crutch and what in the world could she write about aside from two limited subjects, the blind and herself? Dr. Bell had urged her to write on great public questions, the tariff, the conservation of natural resources and how to reform the system of education, but she had little to say about these large matters. In addition to her few books, she wrote articles and essays, and she was grateful to Anne who obliged her to rewrite everything over and over until it conformed to her own idea of style. For Anne had developed a fine taste and a feeling for good English. But people were not interested in anything Helen had to say,—or so she was convinced,—aside from herself, a theme on which editors constantly urged her to write. But on that theme she felt she was written out.

What could she do, then?—obviously, lecture, if she

could learn to speak so that people understood her; and for this purpose she set to work with redoubled perseverance at the old task of struggling for a good voice. She toiled away with a singing teacher, trying to develop her vocal chords so that she could be heard, at least, on a lecture-platform; and she was never to forget the first appearance that she made, in 1913, at Montclair, New Jersey. She might have been standing in a pillory, "cold, riveted, trembling, speechless," feeling that her voice was diving to the lower depths or, as she felt, rising to a queer falsetto, though, among the strong vowel sounds and the carefully uttered consonants,—one auditor said,—some phrases rang out clear. The time came, indeed, when there were many who understood virtually everything she said. This was the result of an effort of twenty-five years. But it left her, nevertheless, with a feeling of frustration. To suggest what she was striving for, her teacher used similes like the rippling of a brook, the full-throated ease of a bird or the notes of a violin or a piano. But, alluring as it was, the goal was beyond her; and, with thousands of unanswered letters piling up around her desk, she could not spend all her time in these vain efforts. She said of this struggle for a natural voice that it "strengthened every fibre of my being and deepened my understanding of all human strivings and disappointed ambitions."

All this meant the end of Helen's dreams of a quiet

life. She soon became accustomed to appearing on platforms, answering questions, intelligent or foolish, asked her by the audience, while Anne gave demonstrations of her teaching. "Do you close your eyes when you go to sleep?" was one of the questions to which she replied, "I never stayed awake to see"; and to the question, "What do you consider the hardest thing in the world?" she answered, "To get Congress to do anything." When she was asked if she could tell colours, she explained that she could not do so by touch but imagined what they were like from poems and descriptions, attaching meanings to them as people attach meanings to terms like hope that cannot be represented by visible objects. For instance, black suggested to her tragedy and evil, as in the "blackness" of misanthropy, melancholy, sin. She liked the question, "What are the characteristics of modern man?" One of these characteristics, she said, was "an intense enjoyment of life, a love of swift movement in aeroplanes, in travel, in dancing," and another was "an appreciation of beautiful simple lines and symmetry, typified by the new buildings and improved city planning." Nor was she averse to the question, "Do you like pretty clothes?" In point of fact, she did, and she always wore them: her teacher had excellent taste in the matter of dress. Anne had noted, when Helen was ten, that she was fond of dress. She had even insisted on having her hair curled when she was too sleepy to stand up.

Anne had noted at the same time that Helen was always attracted to men and made friends with men sooner than with women.

When, for short periods, during four years, 1920-'24, Helen and Anne appeared in a vaudeville circuit, some of their friends remonstrated,—how could Helen permit herself to share a stage with acrobats, dogs and monkeys? It seemed to them deplorable that she could lend herself to this kind of theatrical exhibition; and they were certain that she was being used by unscrupulous persons, like Henry James's charming Verena Tarrant. Her only reply to this was that it was all her own idea and that, as a matter of fact, she enjoyed it hugely, while Anne hated the noise, the rush, the glare; moreover, her act was dignified and it paid better than lecturing or writing and promised to raise a good fund for her teacher's protection. She added in her journal that ever since she was seventeen she had arranged her own life and looked after herself, working very hard for the money she had earned, and, in spite of this, there were still those who appeared to think it incumbent on them to alter her life according to their ideas. She was not interested in watching her steps to please "unadventurous people to whom the untrodden field" was "full of traps and pitfalls," and she had followed her own path,—stubbornly, as many thought,—about the religion of Swedenborg and socialism also. She had gone to college against the advice of all her friends, who told her it would never be worth the effort, and she had studied articulation against the advice even of Anne, who felt the experiment could only disappoint her. When Andrew Carnegie offered her a pension and she said she was a socialist, and he said he would like to spank her for it, her reply was, "A great man like you should be consistent. You believe in the brotherhood of men, in peace among nations, in education for everybody. All those are socialist beliefs." Helen was used to plain speaking and dealing, just as, self-reliant as she was, she packed her own bags in her travels through the country and later through the world. As for the question of vaudeville, she might have said that, in those years, there were other distinguished people appearing in it, among them Madame Schumann-Heink, Carl Sandburg and the naturalist and artist Ernest Thompson Seton.

First or last, Helen Keller appeared in all of the forty-eight states, lecturing also over the Canadian border, in a full glare of publicity from which she was scarcely ever to escape, attended by photographers and reporters. "Ever we move as in a show," she sometimes repeated to herself, quoting the Rubáiyát of Omar Khayyám. She spoke in big noisy tents, crowded with curious country people, in town halls, churches, camps on the edges of lakes, visiting mill towns, mining towns and meat-packing towns with men on strike that brought her closely in touch with the industrial system. She travelled in California, in Oregon, in Washington, guessing where she was by the fragrance of the fruit, the special fruit that marked each particular region, and she criss-crossed other states on early morning milk-trains, riding all night in day-coaches and delivered with the milk. The train stopped on the way at barns where the milk waited in tall bright cans and cheerful young farmers called out greetings to the train-men, while Anne's fingers described for her the exquisite spring foliage and the cows knee-deep in young grass which she could smell. She felt she could see the loveliness of the apple trees in blossom. Going through flooded districts of Texas and California, she felt the water beating against the coaches and the sudden jolt when the train struck a floating log or possibly a dead horse or cow. Once an uprooted tree was caught on the nose of the loco-motive and carried half a mile along the track. At first, while travelling, she found it difficult to get her bearings here and there and she had the same feeling of remoteness that she experienced at sea. But she learned to enjoy the rhythmic vibration of the train and found rest in its swift and steady motion.

It was during one of her vaudeville tours that Helen met Sophie Tucker, who taught both Anne and herself the art of make-up, taking her into the dressing-rooms of some of the other performers so that she could feel their costumes and discuss their work. All this took her back to the days when Ellen Terry,

Sir Henry Irving and "Rip van Winkle" Jefferson
had acted for her. She was happy to have entered
another realm of life, and she was happy to encounter
Sophie Tucker later. This was on shipboard when
Sophie Tucker, who had been kind to her, asked
her to visit the New York night-club, and there she
found herself suddenly with a spot-light turned on
her announcing that Helen Keller was at one of the
tables. Sophie Tucker said, for the audience to hear,
"I hope you haven't found my songs too naughty,"
and Helen stood up and replied, "How could anything be naughty that gives joy to so many people?"
Was it also during the vaudeville years that she met
La Argentina, the dancer, whom she watched from
one of the boxes, catching the mood and the rhythm
of the dances, exclaiming "Wonderful!" again and
again as she followed her companion's eager fingers?
"I knew through my ten eyes," Helen wrote, "how
she wrought into her steps and gestures the tossing of
lily buds in a breeze and the flutter of a dove." Afterwards, in her dressing-room, La Argentina showed
Helen the gowns she had worn as a princess and a
maiden about to be married. When Helen herself
was on the stage, Carl Sandburg wrote to her, "Dear
Helen Keller, I saw and heard you last night and
enjoyed it a thousand ways. The surprise was to find
you something of a dancer, shifting in easy postures
like a good blooded race-horse. Those who see and
hear you feel the zest for living, the zest you vibrate,

is more important than any formula about how to live life."

Helen met Charlie Chaplin too, "a sincere thoughtful young man," she wrote, "deeply interested in his art and his violin," who showed her his nondescript hat and shoes in his studio at Hollywood where he was acting *Shoulder Arms*. In fact, he proposed to break in and wake the "sleeping beauty" in a film in which she herself was supposed to act, during her days of what she called a "would-be star" in Hollywood when she had felt "solemn and clumsy." For in 1918 a plan was on foot for making a movie of the story of her life and she had spent several weeks in Hollywood. There every morning, with her companion, she had gone for a horseback ride, at sunrise, on the trails of Beverly Hills, where she was thrown one day into a strawberry patch when her horse slipped the saddle and galloped off. The film, called *Deliverance*, was supposed to dramatize her life, but, as there was so little drama in this, the producers invented for her absurd adventures. They planned a grotesque and ludicrous banquet assembling her old friends Dr. Holmes, Phillips Brooks, Joseph Jefferson, Alexander Graham Bell, and then she was expected to go to France, during a conference of the Big Four, and urge them to bring the war swiftly to an end. She was asked to be a Joan of Arc, fighting for the workers of the world; she was asked to be a mystical mother of sorrows, grieving for the wounded and the blind;

she was sent up in an aeroplane and then the plan
was changed again and she was supposed to relive the
adventures of Ulysses. Or, rather, she was expected
to show what these adventures meant to her, perhaps
with Ulysses as her lover, for a movie was incomplete
without an interest of the heart. Finally, the producers
introduced a fight, on her behalf, between Ignorance
and Knowledge. A spot was chosen up in the hills
and the hideous giant Ignorance wrestled with the
pale lady Knowledge for the infant Helen. It was
clear to the dullest, after this, that there was no limit
to what might be wrought, as Helen wrote later, into
the Helen Keller picture.

Helen had been meeting and talking to strangers
ever since she was eight years old, and, although she
always found it difficult at first, she acquired Walt
Whitman's philosophy of the "open road." His lines
about knowing the world as a road, about "roads for
travelling souls," mirrored her own inner experience, she said, while she felt like a young spruce tree,
often transplanted, with its roots kept in a ball so that
it could adapt itself to any new place. She learned
with Whitman, as she wrote, "to gather the minds of
men out of their brains" and "to gather the love out
of their hearts" when she met them, and she encountered on these tours some of the largest hearts and
brains that were to be found in the country. The
larger they were, moreover, in one way or another,
the more they were drawn to her, as a general thing,

and Caruso might have spoken for them all when he
said to her, "I have sung the best in my life for you,
Helen Keller." What he had sung was the lament
from *Samson Agonistes,* "wave after wave," as she said,
"into my hand," where his voice "rolled like a river."
In Los Angeles, Chaliapin placed her left hand on
his face as he chanted the *Volga Boat Song* for her,
encircling her with his arm so that she could feel every
vibration when he shouted other humorous folk-songs.
She felt his tone of defiance and his big Russian
peasant's laugh. In Denver, Heifetz played a song
of Schumann for her, with her fingers touching his
violin, and she placed her hands on the piano while
Godowsky played for her one of Chopin's nocturnes.
All of them felt, in her presence, wonder, compassion,
tenderness and awe, and many of them also felt, with
Alexander Woolcott, that she was "just about the
best audience in the world." More than anyone else,
she made them conscious of their own power or perhaps of the possibilities latent in them. For this
reason Harpo Marx was "only too eager to perform
for her," as Alexander Woolcott said on one occasion,
after watching her at the theatre when "her laugh,"
as he recalled, "joyous as an outburst, led all the
rest." For, "through senses we have lost or never
known, she, in perception and appreciation," was "just
a hair's breadth ahead of the rest of the house."

Along with musicians and actors, all manner of
men were drawn to her, and Helen who, as a little

girl, had known the old poets Whittier and Holmes,
attracted many other poets. Carl Sandburg recited
his poems to her, or she read them from his lips,
touching the rim of his guitar as he played it to her,
and Robert Frost praised her in a poem for being

> but more free to think
> For the one more cast off shell.

This appeared in a "Helen Keller anthology," the
work of about seventy poets, among them John Gould
Fletcher, Witter Bynner, Langston Hughes and Coun-
tee Cullen. Then one day Rabindranath Tagore came
out to see her and talked to her about poetry, India
and China. Serene, with his long silky beard, Tagore,
in a circle of reverent listeners, had for her the air
of a biblical prophet, and she placed her hand lightly
on his lips as he recited *In My Garden.* On another
occasion, at a public dinner, she sat by Gerhart
Hauptmann, who was unable to speak a word of
English, while he responded volubly when she broke
the ice by quoting from Goethe's *Hermann und
Dorothea.*

But Helen, interested in all things human, was interested in inventions too, in the smelting of iron,
coal-mining, horticulture, in compasses, bridge-build-
ing, aviation, and, while it amused Henry Ford to
take her through his plant at Detroit, Edison asked
her to visit his laboratory. Edison, however, was blunt
with her and said her voice was "like steam ex-

ploding,"—he could only hear her consonants, being deaf himself. More than once she saw Colonel Roebling, the great designer of Brooklyn Bridge, an invalid, and old, living at Trenton, and Luther Burbank showed her his experimental gardens at Santa Rosa where she saw plants that had never been known before. He put her hand on a thorny cactus and showed her, beside this, the edible thornless cactus he had made from it. Senator La Follette, meeting her, said, "When people meet you, I am sure they always shake hands twice"; and this was the way that Helen Keller felt herself when she encountered Albert Einstein. She was happy when he said to Anne Sullivan, "Your work, Mrs. Macy, has interested me more than any other achievement in modern education. You not only imparted language to Helen Keller but you unfolded her personality; and such work has in it an element of the superhuman." In the large fraternal aura of Einstein's presence, Helen suddenly felt as if earth's discords had been muted, as if a new world had filled this old one just as the spring sun fills a winter sky.

VI

FOR THE BLIND

IN 1917, after living at Wrentham for thirteen years, Helen and Anne Sullivan Macy sold the house there, and they bought a smaller house at Forest Hills, Long Island, from which they could reach New York in a few minutes on the train. They planted trees and vines about this dwelling, where a study was rigged up for Helen in the attic. John Macy was absent more and more,—with John Reed in Europe some of the time,—but Miss Polly Thomson had joined the household in 1914 as Mrs. Macy's assistant and secretary. She had come to America from Glasgow the previous year to visit one of her uncles who was living at Swampscott, and Helen taught her the manual alphabet at once. Quite as remarkable in her way as either of the others, she was to outlive Anne by many years,—replacing her as Helen Keller's alter ego,— and meanwhile, with her aesthetic sense and her diplomatic and practical sense, she became at once an indispensable member of the trio. For the first time there was someone in the house who understood bank accounts and who could read time-tables and map out schedules.

For the rest, John Macy was sometimes there,—

difficult as his position was, as the object of an affection both real and divided,—and there came many of his radical friends, John Reed, Carlo Tresca, Arturo Giovannitti and Big Bill Haywood. There came Margaret Sanger, too, and Flavio Venanzi, with whom Helen was studying Italian. Politics had always interested her; she had read every incoming President's message since the days when she was a schoolgirl preparing for college; and this interest had been so strong even when she was twelve years old that Michael Anagnos had been puzzled by it. When he asked her whether she was a Republican or a Democrat, she had replied, "I am on the fence. I must study civil government, political economy and philosophy before I jump." Later, after studying all these matters, she had become convinced of the rightness of the socialist point of view, and, regarding the "essence of government" as "public welfare," she was always to remain, substantially, of this opinion. She had burning memories of the East Side slums, which she had visited as a child with her teacher and Alexander Graham Bell, and she had seen as a grown woman the dreadful back alleys of Washington and Pittsburgh. Closely following the Lawrence strike, she had been all for the workers, believing that the plants should belong to the producers of the goods, and, concerned for the submerged tenth about whom she wrote an essay, she felt that socialism alone could solve these problems. She delighted in the victory of the International Seamen's Union, correcting the brutalities that had been inflicted on the sailors, and she sympathized heartily with John L. Lewis, rejoicing in the defiant skill with which he had mobilized the miners.

These were still the days of Debs, when the majority of imaginative minds were actively stirred on behalf of the underdog, before the terms "do-gooder," "world-improver," "reformer" and the like had become,—in the words of David Reisman,—terms of contempt. Helen Keller could not share the fatalism of later times when the intellectuals felt with Robinson Jeffers that they were "all compelled, all unhappy, all help-less," and that the wish to "do good" was simply naive; for she had experienced in her own person the power of the will and she felt that to spread well-being was both feasible and right. All her life she grieved over the catastrophes that filled the news,— dust-storms in the middle West, floods in Missis-sippi,—and she instinctively hated the unjust and the cruel. She understood George Orwell's defence of the so-called "materialism" of the working classes, their realization that the belly comes before the soul, not in the scale of values but in point of time; and with this understanding she wrote the essays in *Out of the Dark* that made her for a while almost a social outcast. She wrote that she had a red flag in her study, and, marching in suffrage parades, she shared the front page with baseball and the President's doings, ac-

cepting the notoriety and even happy in it when she
felt that it brought socialism to people's attention.
Naturally, the rumour went about that she was ex-
ploited by the "bolsheviks," for how could this "sweet
girl graduate" who might have stepped out of a poem
of Tennyson lend herself to the abhorrent cause of
revolution? The respectable newspapers said that poor
blind Helen Keller was being used by the socialists
for the sake of her prestige and that, in any case, being
both blind and deaf, she was especially liable to error.
In point of fact, she was independent, for John Macy
did not talk socialism as much as she wished him to
do and Anne was not, at first, a socialist at all.

Following her convictions, Helen Keller advised
college girls to study the problems of mill-hands and
workers in mines and, generally, the living conditions
in industrial cities, relating their knowledge of philosophy and history to the processes that were making
history daily. When Dr. Fosdick, defending the
workers, added that those at the top lacked imagination but were not "bad," she wrote in her journal
presently, "I wonder. . . . I know some lovable per-
sonalities that walk serenely in the vineyards of
abundance with no comprehension of economics."
But she knew others who had seen and felt the
wretched conditions of the toilers, yet clung "with
hidebound selfishness" to things as they were; and,
knowing this, she had been glad to write a preface
for Giovannitti's poems, *Arrows in the Gale*. She

wished to defend her friend and comrade, one of the leaders of the Lawrence strike, feeling that he was, like Shelley, a poet of revolt against cruelties that never should be borne. For her, Giovannitti symbolized "the struggle of a new world against the old world of customs blindly obeyed . . . The seeds of the socialist movement," she added, "are being scattered far and wide, and the power does not exist in the world which can prevent their germination." It was these beliefs of Helen Keller that caused her books to be publicly burned in front of the Berlin operahouse in 1933, while Dr. Paul Goebbels addressed the students who piled them up with other books in the presence of forty thousand persons.

Helen Keller was well aware that poverty and ignorance are often the fundamental sources of blindness, and, in fighting for radical changes in society, she was fighting also for the cause to which she was to devote the rest of her life. She regretted that she could not work for both the blind and the deaf,—and she regarded deafness as the worse misfortune; but, obliged as she was to confine herself to one of these causes alone, she had set to work years before to study it. She had gone in 1904 to the St. Louis exposition to appeal for the education of handicapped people; and, as she thought of the problem that blindness created, she grieved over the multiplicity of prints for the blind. What confusion it produced to have five kinds of raised print in all of which the Bible

had appeared,—Moon type and Boston Line Letter,
New York Point, American braille and European
braille! Knowing them all herself, she exclaimed,
"A plague upon all these prints!" while she deplored
the "American fever of invention," wishing there had
been only European braille. For this was the most
readily adaptable to many different languages, and
even Greek could be embossed in it. Meanwhile, she
realized what a burden were the blind to other
people,—feeling what a "stumbling-block" she was
herself, "a handicap, a hindrance, a tremendous burden"; and she never tired of pointing out that the
minds of the blind could be developed and that their
hands could be trained for their own support. There
were no hopeless blind, she said, among those who
knew braille and who had some kind of work to do.
One problem was the prevention of blindness among
newly born children, caused often by venereal diseases
that were not openly discussed; and, knowing that
in two-fifths of cases blindness was preventable, she
was determined to break this cowardly silence. In
order to do so, she had written as early, as 1907 an
outspoken article for a woman's magazine.

Within a few years after she had served on a Massachusetts commission for the blind, similar commissions
were established in thirty other states; and it was she
who organized the great concert at the Metropolitan
Opera-house to raise funds for starting the American
Foundation for the Blind. That was in 1921, and

after that her chief life work was raising funds for the Foundation. In three years she addressed two hundred and fifty meetings in churches, synagogues, town halls, women's clubs, travelling all over the country, holding out her tin cup, with little taste for the role of a dedicated beggar. It was not easy or pleasant to reiterate endlessly, in articles, messages and letters, the needs of the blind, to explain these to the seeing and to explain as well the best ways of repairing broken lives. It required the utmost care and concentration, for she well knew that a single inept phrase might spoil the whole effect of a speech or a letter. She had, moreover, to avoid the platitudes that, as she was aware, bred irony and doubt. She was obliged to read, or to have read to her, material on the methods by which these problems were handled in England, Germany, Italy and France, while she could scarcely struggle through the floods of mail that came to her from doctors, teachers and parents of handicapped children. Lobbying in Washington, she walked through miles of corridors in the hope of capturing a senator who would champion the blind. More and more the afflicted and the crippled clung to Helen Keller, and, above all, the "loneliest people in the world," her phrase for the deaf-blind who "stared into the dark with nothing but the dark staring back" and whom she was not always able to reach and help.

From the time when she was a little girl, Helen

Keller had seen herself, objectively, as a spokesman for the blind, and when, at eleven, she described in *St. Nicholas* how blind children wrote she had found herself instinctively thinking for them all. They had all kept their lines straight by writing over a grooved board, pressing the paper into the grooves, making the small letters in the grooves while they extended the capitals above and below. This objectivity, or this impersonality, explained why she herself was never spoiled, why, as Ralph Barton Perry put it, she was never "corrupted by kindness" and even ceased to think of her deprivations. Or, at least, as she wrote in one of her books, they no longer saddened her as they had saddened her once in moments of rebellion when she had sat at life's shut gate fighting down the passionate impulses of her nature. She had sometimes felt like a music-box with all the play shut up inside, and she had feared that her limitations unfitted her altogether for the world of men. But, having found her proper work, she asked for no other blessedness, and this enabled her to understand how work could rescue others from their "night of thwarted instincts and shackled ambitions." She had found too how naturally, on every plane of experience, caring for the lives of others enlarged one's own, whether it was Tommy Stringer's life or the life of the blind Texas girl or the life of the Polish boy in Paris. What could be found for each of them to do?

The blind for her were a sort of confraternity and she had blind correspondents all over the world, Olga Skolodhovka, for instance, the Russian poet who was also deaf, and the deaf-blind Madame Berthe Galeron. Victor Hugo had written a preface for the poems of this French friend of hers whom he had called "La Grande Voyante." Meanwhile, it pleased Helen Keller to think of the other great exceptions of whom she wrote in her own preface to *A Challenge to Darkness,* the life-story of a French soldier, J. Georges Scapini, who had been blinded in the first world war. Determined, he said, to get out of life "accomplishment and happiness," he had become a member of the Chamber of Deputies, like the blind American Senator Gore or the blind Tennessean who had founded in London the Academy of Music for the Blind. This Dr. F. J. Campbell had educated there some of the best musicians in England, and, as a mountaineer, to show what the blind could do, he had climbed Mont Blanc on one of his vacations.

It relieved the terrors of blindness to think of its triumphs, and Helen Keller enumerated some of the famous blind like King John of Bohemia who fell fighting at Crécy. Another blind man, John de Trocznow, had led to victory the army of the Hussites, and then there were all the blind minstrels and poets, from Homer and Ossian to Milton, and the Greek rhapsodists who recited heroic poems. The teacher of Cicero was blind, and so was the teacher

of St. Jerome and the teacher of Confucius long
before him. There was John Stanley, the blind com-
poser of Handel's time, and Saunderson who detected with his finger a counterfeit coin that deceived
a connoisseur's eye, Leonard Euler, the Swiss astronomer, and the blind postmaster-general of England who
had first introduced the parcel post. The blind
naturalist Huber had laid the foundations of modern
apiarian science. Speaking of Thierry, the blind
historian, Helen Keller might have referred to Francis
Parkman as well and the American Prescott, who had
cheered himself in his own blindness by drawing up
in an essay a similar list. He had done this to cele-
brate the incorporation in 1830 of the New England
Asylum for the Blind, and he had spoken of Male-
branche who, to think intensely, had closed his shut-
ters closely in the daytime. Prescott repeated the
story of Democritus who was supposed to have put
out his own eyes in order to philosophize the better,
although it was also said that he preferred blindness
to seeing how the wicked continued to thrive. Prescott, who was famous for his own feats of memorizing,
observed that blindness favoured concentration of the
mind, and, speaking again of the blind, he said their
proverbial cheerfulness seemed to prove that deafness
was a far more serious affliction. Helen Keller herself
had found it so.

Prescott had known long before what few had been
aware of, that the blind could be trained to be self-

supporting, and Helen Keller, knowing this, was conscious of the sad results that sometimes came from dwelling on these great exceptions. It was true, there were many instances of blind historians, economists, statesmen, mathematicians, journalists, editors and teachers, but it required a fighting spirit and a forceful personality for a blind person to succeed in these difficult professions. What was more generally called for was to teach the blind to see with their hands as carpenters, wood-workers, weavers, chair-makers, masseurs, or as yacht-builders, road-builders, piano-tuners, tea-tasters, organists or singers. But indeed there were countless lucrative outlets for them. Helen Keller, speaking as one who knew every step of the path, saw it as part of her task to stimulate them, to humanize, as far as she could, the conditions of their lives while kindling a creative sun amid their physical disasters.

VII

"MY RELIGION"

HELEN KELLER had been converted quite early in her life to the mystic Emanuel Sweden-borg's New Church doctrines, a faith that had come to her as naturally, she said, as Conrad had found in English the language of his choice. In this she was alone in her own household, for John Macy was a sceptical rationalist and Anne Sullivan Macy had "no religion at all," as one of their friends put it. Anne had veered both ways in regard to her native Catholicism and these two feelings had cancelled each other out. The Macys thought of Swedenborg as a great man gone crazy, and when Helen Keller referred to him Anne rebuked her, saying, "You know perfectly well you're talking moonshine." But, nevertheless, she read to Helen what Balzac and Coleridge, Emerson and Howells had written about the Swedish seer whose doctrines for Helen herself were anything but moonshine. To her this faith was quite as real as it was to Vachel Lindsay or the landscape painter George Inness or the elder Henry James.

Deeply religious by nature, she had been instructed as a little girl by the singularly undogmatic Phillips Brooks, after whom she had named her infant brother;

but, while she had never had any doubts about God or immortality, she had been baffled by the Bible. She could make nothing of the Apocalypse with its war between God and horned beasts, nor could she associate the eternal torture of those cast into the lake of fire with the God whom Christ identified with love. She had never been drawn to Catholicism, while Newman's *Apologia* had led her to question Protestantism also, and she felt that true religion was obscured by sects and rites and that faith ceased at the approach of orthodoxy. Feeling with Pascal the "enormous difference between piety and goodness," she could not believe in ceremonies that did not have for their object the welfare of mankind, and she had been prepared for a practical religion that saw in the "love of use" the "perfection of man." This she had found in Swedenborg who interpreted the Bible in a way that did not conflict with philosophy or science, whose commentaries did not belie biblical research and who wished to fill with new wine the old vessels of religion.

It was John Hitz, the secretary of Alexander Graham Bell, who had unfolded the doctrines of Swedenborg to her,—the "picturesque secretary," as he was called, with the flowing cape and the long white beard, who had served in Washington as the Swiss consul-general. He had become the superintendent of the Volta Bureau, which collected information about the blind. Helen had first met her "spiritual

godfather" in the capital in 1893, when he took her
to see his old friend Clara Barton, and on her four-
teenth birthday he had given her a watch with raised
hands that enabled her to "feel" the time. There
were gold points indicating the hours around the
rim. This watch had belonged to a German ambassa-
dor who had had to tell the time without consulting
it openly on various occasions, when, during audiences,
he knew he could not stay too long or had to keep
promptly some other appointment. For this he had
had the watch specially constructed. It worked so
well for Helen Keller that later the American Foundation for the Blind adopted a policy of presenting
a similar watch to every man blinded in the war who
returned for treatment. It had been discovered that
as soon as men could tell the time they began to ad-
just themselves to a sightless existence.

After their meeting in Washington, John Hitz often
visited Helen, in Cambridge and later in Wrentham
every summer, and there, as an old man of eighty who
looked much like Walt Whitman, he spent hours
walking with Helen in the country. In his loose
clothes, with his velvet cap, his pockets filled with
needles and thread, safety-pins, thimbles, bandages,
spectacles and books, he spelled his German into her
hands, constantly talking Swedenborg, a copy of whose
Heaven and Hell, in braille, he gave her. The others
thought him a great bore, but not so Helen. He had
learned braille in order to copy out for her bio-

graphical sketches, poems and studies of nature, and he had spent hundreds of hours making extracts for her from other works by the seer whom they both loved. "The spiritual world offers no difficulty," Helen wrote later, "to one who is deaf and blind. Nearly everything in the natural world is as vague, as remote from my senses as spiritual things seem to the minds of most people"; and she soon found that with Swedenborg's help she could dig out of the Bible many precious truths that had escaped her. Thereafter, indeed, she so constantly read it that there were numbers of pages on which her fingers rubbed off all the dots, and she had to supply from memory many verses. For, as she said, Swedenborg, who had "not made a new Bible," had "made the Bible all new" to her; and she was pleased to hear what happened when the Gideon Bibles were removed from a certain large hotel. The next night two hundred enquiries were made for the Bibles.

For it was Swedenborg's mission, as he had seen this himself, to explain to mankind the "spiritual sense" of the Bible, to extricate from the literal the universal sense, the "internal sense" that he called "angelic wisdom." His object was to make Christianity a living reality upon earth, correcting what he considered the erroneous views of the orthodox who had followed the letter of the Bible. For him it expressed in terms of allegory the spiritual history of the human race: it was all a glorious parable and he had seen in it the God of all nations and all times, not merely of the Jews. He did not believe that Genesis and Exodus had anything to do with historical facts, the physical creation of the world or a literal deluge: they stood for the stages of human evolution in which the mind of man developed out of chaos. In the same way the departure from Egypt stood for the exodus of man from his original ignorance and bondage to matter, with his slow difficult progress towards a better life, represented by the fertile land of Canaan. Swedenborg, as his followers thought, had set himself the task of separating the dross from the gold in the Bible, and he had found in it the most important record of the gropings of the human spirit that mankind possesses. His reading of Scripture, moreover, was one that would never be found to conflict with geology, archæology or the progress of historical knowledge.

The upshot of Swedenborg's teaching was that the essence of divine life is love and that men are dead unless they are animated by it. Without love they are in a state of spiritual death, while abandonment of self is another name for heaven and self-will is the cause of the torment of hell. All this was obvious to Helen Keller, and there was nothing incredible for her in Swedenborg's journeys into the other world, which to him was no less actual than this one. For she had experienced the state of inward joy that so many mystics knew as the "honey of the soul," and

she too, like Swedenborg, had had her "illumination,"
a second "birth into life" out of mere existence.
Swedenborg's experience of earth and his contacts
with an immaterial realm were no more irreconcilable
than the two planes of her own life before and after
her awakening to love and knowledge. To her it
seemed natural enough, for the rest, that Jesus should
stand for Divine Love. She was convinced, in short,
that Swedenborg had found "the word of God . . .
freed from the blots and stains of barbarous creeds."
So she wrote in *My Religion.*

No doubt there were other elements in the gospel
according to Swedenborg that appealed to her sense
of beauty or her sense of humour. For instance, his
doctrine of odours must have amused the mind of one
who had such a well-developed olfactory sense. To
Swedenborg all persons threw off "spiritual effluvia,"
and those whom he called the "infernals" loved
stenches: they could not bear the odours of fruit,
frankincense, flowers or bread which appertained
to the spheres of charity and faith. He observed that
one of the heavenly odours was that of good bread,
freshly baked. In general, Swedenborg said that spirits
had an exquisite sense of odours, while one could
characterize almost every human type from the odour
that emanated from it. The sordidly avaricious smelt
like mice, while persecutors of the innocent smelt like
lice, the revengeful and the cruel had a cadaverous

stench and those who studied eloquence to further their own vanity had an odour like the odour of burnt bread. Helen Keller must have understood why Swedenborg loved his garden on the rocky islet of Södermalm, in the outskirts of Stockholm, where he said that in working over his flowers he had often been aware of what their heavenly origin had been. To him a rose was not merely a rose: it was an earthly expression of a celestial emotion. As for his doctrine that those who lived "in heavenly love from affection for truth" spent their spirit-life, in a bright light, on beautiful mountains, in a perpetual springtime, there was in Helen Keller something that recalled it. Otherwise she could not have written, "All about me, in the spirit, is music and brightness, and colour flashes through all my thoughts."

For the rest, she could have said what another Swedenborgian, the elder Henry James, said of himself, that, "having learned the nature of evil, and admitted its power," he himself "turned to the sun of goodness."

* * ǁ

Meanwhile, the health of Anne Sullivan Macy had been slowly giving way. She was beset by illness in one form or another, threatened with tuberculosis and down with influenza, while year by year her eyes grew weaker and weaker. She had always known that sooner or later she would be blind again, and indeed before her death she was to become so. In Helen's life, twice, long before, illnesses of Anne had caused emotional crises, one of them tragic.

The two had been on tour together, lecturing at Bath in Maine, when Anne was suddenly stricken with influenza, and Helen fell into a panic in their rooms at the hotel because she could not use the telephone. She could not communicate with the clerks in the office nor could she find her own way downstairs, and, when at last the two were able to set out for home again, Helen was constrained to appeal to Andrew Carnegie. Bent on maintaining her independence, she had refused the pension that he had offered to bestow on her, and she felt now that she was obliged to accept it. To be sure, it was not large enough to pay more than half their expenses,—she was no more able than willing to give up her work. But at least it relieved a situation that had left her more insecure than ever. For she could no longer count on her teacher's help.

A far more serious crisis arose when the household for a time was broken up and Anne was sent away to the Adirondacks, only to go off again, directly from Lake Placid, this time with Polly Thomson to Puerto Rico. The tour that summer had been exhausting, and Helen, left with her mother in the house, was overwhelmed by a sense of her isolation. She was afraid that destiny was going to take Anne away from her, and she planned, in case this happened, to elope with a young newspaperman who had served as an interpreter during the tour. The young man in question was living in the house, acting, in Miss Thomson's absence, as a secretary, reading to Helen every day, talking to her and walking with her in the splendour of the Wrentham autumn woods. Then, full of plans for her happiness, he asked her to marry him, and he and Helen took out a marriage license. Helen had been on the point of telling her mother and Anne about it when a meddlesome reporter dug out the story, and the newspapers were full of it the following day. Mrs. Keller, horrified and angry, carried Helen off to Alabama.

As Helen wrote later, "The love which had come, unseen and unexpected, departed with tempest on his wings"; and this brief love remained in her life "a little island of joy surrounded," as she said, "by dark waters." She told the story in *Midstream,* which continued the tale of her life since she had left college. She had written *My Religion* just before this larger work, together with a preface for a volume of Swedenborg in braille, typing away in her Forest Hills attic and bringing down fragments of her work for her companions to spell back to her and put together. Meanwhile, Anne's declining health obliged them to take time off and escape from the torrent of letters that poured down upon them. One summer they had a real vacation, camping out for two months, with a car and tents, in a pasture in the Berkshires, then in a pine wood near Lake Champlain and a hay-field near Montreal and finally in Maine on the Kennebec river. Helen delighted in the hill roads, fragrant with moss and wet grass, and the deep valley roads, all of them so narrow that the bushes touched her as she passed.

Some time later, in 1933 and 1934, they spent a whole sabbatical year in Europe, preceded by trips in earlier years to Brittany, Cornwall and Ireland, where they looked for traces of Anne's forbears. They picnicked near Killarney on the spot on which Daniel O'Connell was born and walked on a rocky spur of the Wicklow mountains, then, for seclusion and absolute quiet,—for Anne had been desperately ill,—they went over to Essex for the rest of the summer. There they rented an Elizabethan cottage. Moving through the winding lanes, they conjured up in fancy the six or more buried civilizations over which they were treading, and the odour of antiquity came off on their hands as they touched the Roman walls and the trenches among which the army of Boadicea was defeated. Earlier still they had stayed in Cornwall in a little fishing village where the low thatched cottages were buried in wistaria and roses and the soft white clouds tumbled over one another in the sky, and where, on their arrival, Helen had jumped out of the car to feel the wild violets in their blue pools. There were wonderful hedges of blackthorn, broom and laurel and the golden primroses raged over the fields, while wild ponies raced up and down the heather-covered hillocks and the clamour of yellow-billed sea-gulls filled the air. This had been Helen's first glimpse of the country of Shakespeare and Wordsworth. The moment they crossed the river Tamar dividing Devon from Cornwall, they had felt as free of their own past as the children of Israel crossing the Jordan from Egypt.

Their object had been to escape the publicity that harassed them at home, where Helen felt like a hunting dog always following some new scent, uncovering and pursuing more dollars for the blind. She was constantly planning another campaign, wherever she happened to be, composing and copying appeals and speeches on the typewriter that accompanied her, with boxes of braille notes for her literary work. Even in England she was besieged by photographers and interviewers, and there was a barrage of telegrams every day; and one summer was interrupted by a summons to Jugoslavia to start there a Helen Keller fund. King Alexander decorated her with the medal of St. Sava, while at Semlin she visited the school for the blind. In London, at a royal garden party, she gave the King and Queen what Anne called a lip-reading demonstration; and, dining at the House of Commons, she met Clement Attlee, who had spent fourteen years in the slums of the East End. Then, at Lady Astor's, she encountered Bernard Shaw, almost all of whose plays she knew and with whom she had longed to talk ever since she had read *Pygmalion*. She had meant to tell Shaw that, staying in London, she had read every night a copy of *The Apple-Cart*, which she kept at her bedside, and she was surprised, when she held out her hand, to find his unresponsive and bristling as much with egotism as a porcupine with quills. His handshake was prickly, not unlike a thistle, the handshake of a man, she said later, whose brain overbalances his heart; and she felt a strange quiver running through Mrs. Macy's hand when her teacher repeated Shaw's remark. Lady Astor had said to him, "You know, Miss Keller is deaf and blind," and he replied, "Why, of course, all Americans are deaf and blind—and dumb." Had he been startled out of a nap? Or was he the victim of his own legend? Was he at that moment Shaw the showman, who had always been expected to shock and astound? Later Shaw said he had never made this strange remark, which, nevertheless, a roomful of others heard. But Helen Keller, surprised, was not seriously offended. She remained grateful to Bernard Shaw for exposing the lies of our civilization and for what she called the wind of scorn with which he swept through shams and pharisaism. He remained for her "the chief prosecutor of his time."

Her own mind was never more alive than when she was in Scotland, a country especially dear to her as Polly Thomson's homeland and the birthplace of Alexander Graham Bell. She was never to forget the

journey on the Flying Scotsman when the engineer
had guided her to his own seat in the locomotive and
she had fed with coal the fiery dragon. Then she
had reached out her hand for the current of air as
the train shot through Berwick-on-Tweed, travelling
at seventy miles an hour. Bothwell, the manse of
Polly's brother, became a second home for her, where
the minister's children, one and all, learned the manual
alphabet to tell her about their doings and ask about
hers. In Scotland one of the universities gave her an
honorary degree, and the Earl of Aberdeen broadcasted
a lecture about her; while, interested in everything,
she learned how to make a tee and how to swing her
arms in the game of golf. She visited a coal-miner's
family up in the hills in a house that recalled the
Cotter's Saturday Night, and she went nine hundred
feet down in a mine-shaft; then she visited the birthplace of one of her heroes, David Livingstone, in a
tenement containing twenty one-room dwellings. She
grieved that all his efforts in behalf of the African
natives had been lost sight of in Europe's greed for
empire. She visited the Shetlands and the Orkneys,
where the fragrance of the clover followed her as she
sailed from island to island, and Anne or Polly, with
flying fingers, tattooed into her receptive palm every
sight and sound along the way. They climbed the
strange mounds of the old Norsemen who had occupied the islands, and they stopped at Skye, the mys-
terious isle of rain, mist and wind, carpeted with

heather and bog-myrtle. The perfume of sweet-brier and fir mingled with honeysuckle pervaded the shadows of the mountains, the deep valleys and the cliffs.

For a Highland holiday, eighteen miles from Inverness, they were installed for a few weeks in a cozy old farmhouse, with an approach through bracken and gorse, tall ferns and meadow-sweet, and with black Angus cattle grazing in the fields. In the evening, after the day's work, they went for walks in the sunset glow through dusky lanes bordered by stone walls mossy with age; but Anne's eyes were rapidly failing there and it became Helen's turn to teach her how to read in the original braille. For Braille's own old system had been restored. There too Anne received sorrowful news. As they had driven up·to the farmhouse they saw a gull, close to the door, that lifted wide wings and flew away, and, when they entered, a telegram was placed in Anne's hand telling her that John Macy had just died. "The dreadful drama is finished," she wrote in a letter to one of her friends who knew what few others had ever guessed, that marriage had all but shattered her house of life, —"the fierce struggle that won only despair." She added, "There is in the most passionate love more pain than joy."

Perhaps Anne was not unaware that she herself had but a short time to live.

VIII
INTERLUDE: ENGLAND AND JAPAN

THE ASHES of Anne Sullivan Macy were placed in the National Cathedral in Washington, not far from the tomb of Woodrow Wilson. The date was November 3rd, 1936; and the Bishop of Washington referred to her in his address as "one of the great teachers of all time."

With Polly Thomson, a few days later, Helen Keller sailed again for the Scotland where she had felt at home, while, as she wrote, "the days ground over" her "as a glacier over a field once joyously green." She had to reintegrate her life, so shocked and lacerated by the wrench of separation from her lifelong companion, and from that moment she was determined to write about her teacher the book that actually appeared nineteen years later. On shipboard now she felt like a somnambulist whom only an intense faith carried forward; but, feeling that life is a wonderful game, she was bent on playing it out to the end, convinced that courage is the cure for every sorrow. Polly, as they walked the deck, described the white sea-swallows that flew thousands of miles over the ocean, small and defenceless as they were, beyond hope of rescue, and these tiny birds circling round the ship

111

awoke in her own mind fresh courageous thoughts. As the hours glided by, life again pulsed through her, and she could already dimly feel her delight in philosophy, poetry and travel reviving.

Long before, when she was a child, her teacher had encouraged her to keep a daily record of her thoughts and her life. Now, beginning to do so, she found it a godsend. The journal, which she published later, helped her, during these critical days, to attune her mind again to the habit of work; and Polly Thomson, who had already been with her for twenty-two years, brimmed over with an eager awareness of their surroundings. She had an actress's talent, besides, for recreating in Helen's hand the pathos, the beauty or the humour of everything she saw,—all day her fingers positively hummed with interest; and, just as on shore, at the theatre or the movies, she rapidly spelled out the dialogue, describing the facial expressions and the costumes of the actors, so she interpreted for Helen the life of the ship. She passed on the story of the Nuremberg zoo, which the German captain told them, when the door of the monkey-house was left unlocked and scores of monkeys ran loose through the streets; while Helen, as earnest and eager as Polly, with her own child-like wonder, noted every footfall on the deck. Always observing, examining, reflecting, she was excited as ever by the huge docks at Southampton and the multitude of ships from all the seven seas loading and unloading, only regretting that she missed so much in conversation, the meanings that looks and tones alone conveyed. How much she too longed to enjoy the flying comments and anecdotes, the sudden quirks and turns that she could not follow!

But, as she wrote in her journal, she rarely thought of her deafness and blindness, or, at least, they had ceased to sadden her, all too conscious as she was of the black clouds threatening Europe; for she foresaw already the war that was coming. She was told that forty million gas-masks were being prepared for England and Scotland alone. The world of 1936-'37 summed itself up in an image for her. It was like a non-stop express train freighted with dynamite; and what a devastating proof it was that social justice had been postponed centuries too long. Even in the quiet Scottish manse that she and Polly visited again she could not escape from the horror of it. Every day at breakfast Polly spelled out the news for her, the story of the Soviet purge that recalled the Salem witchcraft trials, the barbarities of the Spanish civil war. She saw Spain as a country where tolerance had always been trampled upon, where there had always been a government founded on force and where the caste system was as rigid as that of India, veiled as it was with poetry and romance. Then there were the atrocities in Germany and the black crimes against genius, the exiling of Einstein. Helen Keller's German publisher had arrogantly told her to alter the text of her *Midstream*, omitting her sympathetic words about the new Russia; but, increasingly aware as she was of the tyranny of the Soviets, she was still more antagonistic to the tyranny of the Nazis. She felt that one had to allow for the Asiatic modes of the Russian mind, remembering also the misery of the earlier Russia; and, as for the godlessness that horrified her too, was this really the result of bolshevism? She was convinced that this godlessness was a consequence of faith long mocked, petitions and cries to heaven that had been answered only by floggings, evictions, increased taxes and persecution. All things considered, she felt sure that Russia was advancing; and she wrote to this German publisher an indignant letter forbidding him either to alter or to publish her books.

More than ever, in Scotland and England, a feeling of wonder swept over her that the British could still be living, on their island, so greatly; and she hoped they might be able to achieve their goal, a commonwealth of trusting free peoples. Every war had for her the horror of a family feud, for she felt that her fatherland was the whole world; so she was happy when she was asked, while she was in England, to unveil in Paris a statue of Thomas Paine. She thought of Paine as a miraculous man who had cleared the way for a world federation of nations, one who had found his kindred in other countries where a narrow patriotism would have obscured his vision. A lonely man, misconstrued and amazingly ignorant, for the rest, he had yet become a chain-breaking, throne-

shaking genius. He had put an end to superstitions
that were not faith but blindness, sheeplike submis-
sion to tyranny and a famine of knowledge as fatal
as physical starvation. So Helen Keller wrote in her
journal.

Meanwhile, always reaching out to meet the minds
of others, she kept her own mind fresh and well-in-
formed, visiting museums and exhibitions and opening
herself to the points of view of all sorts and conditions of men and women. Interested in books as well,
she read Kenneth Grahame's *The Wind in the Wil-
lows,* together with E. V. Lucas's *A Wanderer in London,* to give her a clearer feeling for the genius of the
city, and she instantly read a new life of Napoleon
that someone recommended, eager to understand this
enigmatic figure. Reading biographies of Gladstone
and Disraeli, she found herself, not for the first time,
preferring the latter, antagonized by Gladstone's "bull-
dog grip on an argument" and his involved periods,
sonorous and vague. She might well have taken for
her own the motto of Disraeli, "Life is too short to
be little." She cared most for books that brought
her close to elemental things, Willa Cather's *My
Antonia* and Hamsun's *The Growth of the Soil,* for
instance, but she also delighted in Conrad's *Youth*
and *Heart of Darkness* and Turgenev's *Smoke* and
Spring Freshets. Meeting Lord Avebury's son, she
was able to tell him that his father's *The Beauties of
Nature* had been one of her favourite books when

she was a child; and she discussed poetry with Clifford Bax. This English playwright was a Buddhist, and with him she compared the teachings of Swedenborg and Buddha, his faith and her own, while he told her that he had first heard of her when she was fifteen and he was a student in Germany, three years older. Together they talked about T. S. Eliot and the Irish poet A E, whose faith in the good will of mankind resembled her own. She could not share Eliot's feeling that men were rotten, and her mind recoiled before the tomblike finality of *The Hollow Men,* although there was no denying the power of the poem. Always responsive to poetry, she was happy later with the romance and richness of expression that seemed to be coming back with Christopher Fry, and she was greatly interested in Robinson Jeffers. She quoted in her journal the lines he had written about a rock cave near Tassajara that contained a prehistoric painting of hands. It seemed to say, Jeffers wrote:

> Look, we also were human; we had hands, not paws. All
>   hail,
> You people with cleverer hands, our supplanters
> In the beautiful country; enjoy her a season, her beauty,
>   and come down
> And be supplanted; for you also are human.

Later she recalled in one of her books how Anne Sullivan had encouraged her to read poetry to put her mind in tune, "to strip off the leaves of a poet's thoughts, expose the fruit to the sun of our own spirits and observe how the flavour is changed by its rays." It was fascinating, Anne Sullivan said, "to watch how the blossoms and fruits of the poet's mind take on different hues, odours and savours when transplanted to another brain." Helen had always kept fresh her own love of poetry. Meanwhile, she noted that the love of travel was growing in her, a wish to see more of the world; and during this visit to England an opportunity came to her in the form of an invitation to visit Japan. Ever since she had seen as a child the World's Fair in Chicago, she had longed to visit this island empire, and the invitation expressed the hope that she might arouse in the Japanese people a nation-wide interest in their own blind. She had been concerned with the frightful prevalence of blindness in the Orient, where a large proportion were to be found of the estimated fourteen million blind people in the world, and she saw in this prospect of work in Japan a kind of weapon for herself against the life-wrecking sorrow of her teacher's death. Thinking of the East, she knew that an appalling belt of darkness extended from Morocco all the way, and she felt it as a challenge to penetrate this darkness and the silence that went with it, scarcely touched by hope. She was convinced that she lived in a redemptive world that had no hopeless continents or islands.

Returning home, she prepared for the voyage and soon set out with Polly, stopping on the way at Honolulu to urge the legislature to provide a board of welfare for the blind of Hawaii. Then, on shipboard, with fear and trembling, she wrote the speeches, ten or twelve, which the staggering programme of the Japanese government called for, disobeying the doctor's orders and working day after day from five o'clock in the morning till ten at night. She had to reiterate the same points over and over, but always with new shades of feeling and new ideas, and she was mentally black and blue from writing and rewriting, trying to pack more and more into the speeches. For much depended on these pleas for the Japanese blind. She was up and out with Polly, rehearsing them before dawn while the sailors were washing down the decks. Betweenwhiles, with the Japanese captain of the ship, she discussed Conrad's tributes to the sailors and the sea, and she read the twelve braille volumes of *Gone With the Wind*. Sometimes she read this on deck, sometimes after she had gone to bed where, under the covers, her fingers brought the story to life. She had so many obligations that she sympathized at moments with the old woman who lived in a shoe, and she found relief in these images of the Southern plantation that brought back so much of her own childhood. They recalled the spring and summer days, the red earth, the magnolia trees, the drowsy afternoons of Alabama, the perfume of the roses, the jessamine, the paulownia blossoms, and she could hear her father and his friends fighting over the Civil War and see the Negroes in their bright-coloured bandannas. Reading the book, she lived again the wonderful days before Christmas when so many pleasant odours filled the house and when, to keep her out of mischief, she had been encouraged to share in the elaborate ritual of the preparations. She remembered the pungent and fragrant ingredients she collected for the fruit-cake without which Christmas would not have been Christmas. She had been allowed to lick the stirring spoons, pick over the raisins and grind the spices.

Lecturing presently all over Japan, she was able to raise for the blind and deaf a sum of thirty-five million yen, appealing to the people four or five times a day to cast off their ancient superstitions about blindness. It struck her that everywhere the two extremes, the old and the modern, were struggling to get the upper hand. She travelled on railroads as a guest of the nation, with the Empress's sister part of the way, with a special cook and two maids provided for Polly and herself, so that they were not even permitted to put on their own shoes. Everywhere they slept in royal apartments, while pathways before them were literally buried in flowers, and the schoolchildren, who gathered in crowds, seemed to know more about Helen Keller than they knew about their own Japanese statesmen. Working for the hand-

icapped, she made history in Japan, aided by her
great friend Takeo Iwahashi, the director of the
Lighthouse at Osaka. Once a student of engineering,
he had gone blind at thirty and had been saved afterwards from hara-kiri; then, sent to Edinburgh, he had
become the principal of a school for the blind in
England. He had returned to his own country to
work for the blind there and adapt the braille system
for the Japanese.

Helen and Polly visited Lake Biwa, where the
ashes of Fenollosa lay, Mount Aso, the inland sea and
Hokkaido; and never had they seen such cascades
of wistaria or heard of so many festivals or such pro-
cessions constantly visiting shrines. At Nara they had
a four-day vacation, in a park girdled with mountains
where the sacred deer roamed unmolested, where,
bounding in the early morning air, they all came
running at the sound of a bugle to be fed. Helen
was the first woman who had ever been permitted
to touch the great bronze Buddha seated on lotus
leaves; and in Tosa province she was photographed
with a famous white bird perched in a tree trail-
ing a tail that was eighteen feet long. This tail
had taken, by cross-breeding, two hundred years to
produce, and the bird remained high in the tree so it
could hang freely. A page boy exercised it for half
an hour every day, holding the tail to keep it from
touching the ground. For the rest, more than once,

Polly had occasion to lament over some of the things a celebrity was expected to do.

In later years Helen Keller was to return to Japan. This was the first of her tours around the world.

IX

AT WESTPORT: JO DAVIDSON

AFTER HER TEACHER'S DEATH, Helen Keller no longer felt that she could live happily at Forest Hills, and she and Polly presently moved to Westport in Connecticut, where they spent a year in the house of Professor Robert Pfeiffer. The uncle of this great biblical scholar, Gustavus Pfeiffer, who lived near by,— a trustee of the American Foundation for the Blind,— presently built a house for them with ample grounds about it where the two installed themselves in 1939. They called the place Arcan Ridge after the Scottish farmhouse where they had spent both sad and happy days and where Helen had been able to walk alone with a shepherd's crook to guide her, scattering crumbs for the pheasants that abounded in the gorse. To her the name signified liberty, among odorous floods of wild roses and broom, for there she had wandered far quite by herself.

At Arcan Ridge too, every day, she went for a walk in the woods, with a German shepherd dog for company, following a cedar guide-rail that was built along a winding path and that stretched a quarter of a mile out from the garden. There was an electric buzzer in the pantry connecting with the study, where Helen

spent most of the day on the second floor; and, pressing this once, twice or thrice, Polly could tell her
when meals were ready or when a guest was waiting
to see her below. She would catch the vibrations on
her desk upstairs and reply with a movement of the
feet, "Coming down." She had remarked in *The
World I Live In* that the tactual silence of the country
was always most welcome to her after the din of town
and the harassing concussions of the train. For her
whole body was alive to the conditions about her, and
the rumble and roar of the city streets, the multitudi-
nous trampling of feet and the clangour of cars and
machinery tortured her nerves. In the country the
thousand soft voices of the earth caressed her, the
small rustle in tufts of grass, the silky swish of leaves,
the hum of the bees in blossoms when she plucked
them. She loved the buzz of insects and the rippling
vibration of water running over pebbles.

Among her Westport neighbours, she especially
delighted in Professor Pfeiffer,—of the Harvard Divin-
ity School,—and his Florentine wife, one of whose
frequent summer guests was Gaetano Salvemini, the
De Bosis Lecturer on Italian Civilization at Harvard.
Salvemini had been for many years, and was to be
again, a professor at the University of Florence, where
his friend Bernard Berenson called him "a prophet
and defender of every good cause" and "the idol of
all that was most cultured in Florentine society." A
survivor of the liberal world of Mazzini, to whose

ideals he tenaciously clung, anticipating the second Risorgimento that was to follow, he hoped, the fall of Mussolini, he had been challenged to a duel by the Duce before he escaped from Italy, where he had been arrested and imprisoned. As a teacher of history, generous, humane, he illustrated the saying of Plutarch that the soul is not a vessel to be filled but a fire to be kindled, and his wish as a writer of history was that he might open up fresh opportunities for furthering well-being and justice. The author of a famous history of the French Revolution, he was writing *Under the Axe of Fascism* at present, a child himself of the eighteenth century that "discovered happiness," as Saint-Just said, whose own motto was "Clarity is the moral integrity of the mind."

To Helen Keller and her circle of friends, the philosophy of this devoted man, this incorruptible sage, was a joy and a blessing, as I, for one, can testify, for I too at about this time became, as a Westport neighbour, one of the circle. It was a pleasure to hear him denounce the retrogression in the United States towards "legitimacy, tradition, symbols and similar nonsense," all the more absurd in a country born from a revolution that was "illegitimate" and "anti-symbolical" also. He added once, "The whole world now is a succession of *Buts.* I am a liberal, *but* . . . I am ashamed of being a liberal. I am a socialist, *but*," for he felt that all these words had been sadly tarnished. What love of Italy led him to say that his countrymen

had "no political sense, no juridical or economic
sense, no common sense," but that they had "a sense
of humanity that makes up for all." When Jo Davidson appeared everyone was happy, and Helen herself
was never more radiantly so than when she was in the
presence of this lovable sculptor. (It was through
him, I should add, that I had met her.) As an art-
student, Jo Davidson had learned the manual alphabet
from a deaf-mute friend who was also a sculptor, and
he could spell into Helen's hand at once. He had
modelled figures of three of her favourites, Thomas
Paine, Whitman and Thoreau, and he had been drawn
to Salvemini instantly also. Living most of the time
in France, and loving it so deeply that he could see
no faults in anything French, he exclaimed one day
that he had never known an Italian or a Frenchman
who had not had an artist as a friend. "Now all you
Anglo-Saxons!" he said defiantly, glaring round, hint-
ing an imperfection in some of the others.

Jo Davidson had scarcely met Helen Keller before
he persuaded Polly and herself to visit his farm in
Pennsylvania and sit for a bust. "As soon as they
stepped across the threshold," he then wrote to me,
"the house was flooded with sunshine." In the studio
the next morning Helen's hand wandered over his
busts and he realized that she was "seeing these por-
traits profoundly," saying, for instance, of Einstein,
whom they both revered, "He is like a sunflower."
Exploring Helen's mind, Jo wrote, was "a rich ad-

venture . . . Thoughts and words were miraculously superimposed on each other with astonishing precision. I realized the profound honesty of her thinking." She, in turn, afterwards wrote to him, as he reported in his autobiography, "Until I came to your studio, I had often seemed to move in a deaf-blind show, but you multiplied my powers of feeling, reflecting and observing as you worked, and now there will be a new significance in whatever there is left for me to accomplish. You confirm the truth which has always burned into me,—spiritual exaltation is not enough. We must also lift our earth-horizon . . . or we shall always profane our high thinking by mean living." (To me she said, after Jo Davidson's death, that he had "lived greatly.")

To Helen Keller, sculpture was the most rewarding of all the arts,—that is to say, after poetry and good prose writing,—for, as she said, in her land of darkness and silence, she could feel its "flowing curves and bendings." In her childhood, at the World's Fair in 1893, the bronzes of Barye's animals had pleased her more than even the Japanese exhibit; and a Boston artist whom she met, seeing her pleasure in sculpture, suggested that she might develop a talent for it. Anne Sullivan, who was always ready for any new discovery, excited by this remark, followed it up, for modelling had never been attempted by a deaf-blind person; so she and Helen both took lessons, first in wax, then in clay. Helen was fascinated by the objects that she could shape, cups and saucers, baskets, fruits and so on, and to please Anne she worked until her hands were exhausted. Anne read into her hands biographies of sculptors to show her their tremendous determination, but Helen finally came to grief with a big artificial uninteresting fern that was far from suggesting the ferns that she felt in the woods. She continued to drudge away, with no results that pleased her, and even in later life she modelled a few heads. But she had always greatly preferred to read.

For the sculpture of others, however, she never lost her active taste, and when she was at Radcliffe the director of the Boston art museum had enabled her to feel the sculptures and the casts. Standing on a stepladder she had explored with her hands the figures of the gods and heroes of Greece and Rome, tracing with her finger-tips every line and curve, discovering the thought and the emotion which the artist had portrayed. There was Diana with her hand by the quiver, Niobe sheltering her youngest child, Laocoön with his sons struggling in the coils of the serpents, and she noted in all their faces the signs of courage, hatred, love, the grace and freedom of the forest in Diana's posture, the bland curves of Venus and this goddess's repose. Her fingers played over the reproductions of the bronze doors of Ghiberti, a foretaste of the pleasure that awaited her in Florence. She asked, "Where are the singers?" in a bas-relief of dancing girls, and, finding them, she said, "One is silent," for she observed that the lips of this girl were closed. As she noted in her book *The World I Live In,* she felt "the sweep of sea-winds" in the robes of the Winged Victory at the museum and "the splendour of conquest in her wings."

"Of course," she had also written, "my fingers cannot get the impression of a large whole at a glance; but I feel the parts, and my mind puts them together." And there was no question that her aesthetic sense was both naturally acute and well-developed. She was happy when a friend passed on to her two sayings of Ghiberti, describing antique sculptures in Padua and Rome,—in one case, "Its more exquisite beauties cannot be discovered by the sight, but only by the touch of the hand passed over it." Of the other sculpture Ghiberti said, "It has very many sweet beauties which the eye alone can comprehend not, either by strong or tempered light; only the hand by touching them finds them out"; and perhaps there were few beauties that Helen Keller failed to find in her lifelong appreciation of the sculptor's art. In Paris she had spent hours at the Rodin Museum, where she was permitted to explore the great dome of Balzac's forehead, the "Grief," the "Victor Hugo" and the "Burghers of Calais." To her this work was "sadder to touch than a grave" because it was "a conquered city typified." As for the "Thinker," she felt in every limb of this the "throes of emerging mind," as she wrote in her journal. She went on to say, "I recog-

nized the force that shook me when Teacher spelled
'water'. . . . Often before had my deliverance caused
me to wonder, but not until then had I perceived
clearly how Teacher hewed my life bit by bit out of
the formless silent dark as Rodin hewed that mind-
genesis out of the rock." (During this visit to Paris,
at a service in the Madeleine, she regretted that the
organ-music did not reach her, for the marble floor
could not transmit the vibrations. Nevertheless, she
captured some of the chords by placing her hand on
a chair.)

It was thus by a natural affinity as lovers of sculpture
that Helen Keller and Jo Davidson were drawn together, while, as lovers also of Whitman and Paine,
they were both citizens of the world and friends of
all that was liberal and humane. Jo, having done a
bust of her, felt he must do a second bust that would
include as well her uplifted hands, for, as he said, her
extraordinary gestures were an important part of her
uniqueness. Everyone who knew her recognized as
characteristic Helen's way of throwing up her hands
in moments of excitement; and Jo noted the clairvoyant nature of these hands with which she explored
lightly the head and face of every new person she
met. She would then comment perhaps on some in-
teresting feature, and, as Jo said, you knew that she
had seen this person and that in the future she
would know him again.

During the second world war, she and Jo Davidson

were often together, when she visited the naval hospital in Philadelphia, for instance, and at President
Franklin Roosevelt's fourth inauguration. Then,
later, in 1950, she and Polly visited Jo and Florence
Davidson at Saché in France. That was her first real
vacation in fifty years, for always before on her travels
she had been constantly occupied with plans for new
campaigns or with speeches at the moment. But here,
in the lovely old manor-house where Jo lived, fourteen
miles from Tours, and only half a mile from the little
château where Balzac had written *Le Lys dans la Val-
lée,* here, at Becheron on the river Indre, she celebrated
her seventieth birthday and Jo painted a portrait of
herself and Polly. He called it a conversation-piece,
for it represented Polly talking, in her lively fashion,
into Helen's hand, while the two posed on the stand
for the model and Jo, behind the big canvas, struggled
with his paint. He struggled with the light too, pull-
ing at his beard, desperate one minute, elated the
next, for he was not quite at home with a brush in
his hand. They all went for walks in the fields, blue
with cornflowers and red with poppies, while larks
flew up suddenly into the sky. It was June and they
visited the cherry trees, gorging themselves on the
fruit, or wandered in the garden, refreshing themselves with strawberries, and once at tea-time Jo said,
"One talks from the heart first," and Helen's mind
flowed with ideas. They dabbled a little in the difficult
French of Rabelais, and Jo reminded Helen, who had

her own jokes too, that Rabelais had been born only
twenty miles away. Polly read H. G. Wells's *Experiment in Autobiography*, while Helen read in braille
Anatole France and *Candide*,—they all seemed to be
reading two or three books at a time. "What a
privilege it has been," Florence Davidson wrote to
me, "to live with Helen and Polly. Every day Helen
delights us more and more—her noble simplicity, her
ability to drink in the feel of things, and that spring
of joyousness which bubbles up to the surface at the
slightest pressure. Jo is at his best with her and though
our troubled times make us sad we have many a merry
meal together."

It was from Becheron that they all drove to Chartres
one day, where Helen's fingers played over some of
the sculpture; and then the Davidsons drove to Genoa,
where Helen and Polly were making a visit, and carried them both over to Florence. Salvemini, who was
waiting for them, had made arrangements for Helen
to see the sculptures of Donatello and the Medici
chapel A movable scaffold was set up so that she
could pass her hands over the works at the Bargello,
where she exclaimed with pleasure as she touched the
open mouth of Donatello's singing "John the Baptist."
When she came upon the Madonna and Child and
discovered the suckling babe, she murmured "Innocent greed." Then they went on to the chapel with
the Medici tombs, and Jo Davidson said he had never
seen these sculptures so intimately as when he watched

Helen's hands wandering over the forms. She peered into every crevice, she felt the subtlest modulations,— she had "ten eyes for sculpture," Salvemini said,— and few could ever have understood better the motives of Michelangelo in wishing to restore the sense of the dignity of man. For no one was more aware than she that men had been stunted and deformed, and she too had always had in her mind the idea of another humanity such as the sculptor had imagined, beautiful and strong.

X

FROM A NOTEBOOK

DURING THESE YEARS at Westport, and after I moved elsewhere, I took occasional notes about Helen Keller, jotting down chance remarks of hers and other memoranda, among them certain comments that she suggested. I offer these, unconnected as they are, as follows:

July, 1944

Helen has been out picking blueberries today. She has only to touch them to know when they are ripe.

The paths and garden at Arcan Ridge are all so perfectly kept that I exclaimed over them. Helen does it. In summer she is up at five every morning, edging the driveway and the paths. She asks Herbert Haas what she should do next. Then she weeds the flower-beds. She distinguishes by touch between the flowers and the weeds.

(Herbert Haas is a good part of the life of the household. He drives the car, he built the hand-rail, he knows the manual alphabet and he copies articles and documents in braille for Helen.)

Helen comes to dinner, bringing her checker-board for a little game.

I had happened on a poem "To Helen Keller" by

Edmund Clarence Stedman, published in 1888, fifty-seven years ago. This poet had written an ode to Lincoln at the time of his death in 1865. Now, half-way through another century, Helen looks at times, and even very often, like a young girl. How many poems were written to her by Robert Frost and others in the far-off days when poetry was still "public."

August

Dinner with Helen and Gaetano Salvemini at Professor Robert Pfeiffer's. Our Florentine hostess Mrs. Pfeiffer played an Italian song. Helen stood by with her left hand on the piano-top, waving gently with her right hand, keeping perfect time. She feels the vibrations through the piano and the floor. In this way she recognizes many compositions.

Someone asked her how she knows the difference between day and night. "Oh," she said, "in the day the air is lighter, odours are lighter, and there is more motion and more vibration in the atmosphere. In the evening quiet there are fewer vibrations. The air is dense and one feels less motion in things."

How did she think of colours? She said she thought of red as warm, and she connected pink with rosebuds and green with young growing plants. Purple means to her deep feeling; yellow means joyousness, gaiety, sunlight; blue means space, distance, airiness, the sky.

Of course, as Polly says, these impressions are drawn from her reading. But what struck me, as Helen talked, was that no colour, except black at times, suggests to her anything negative or sad. Occasionally black evokes, for

her, misanthropy and the idea of sin. But it also calls
up the feeling of solitude and peace, and I remember in
connection with this something she once wrote: "To the
blind child the dark is kindly. In it he finds nothing
extraordinary or terrible. It is his familiar world." As a
rule, her associations are naturally happy.

September, 1944

With Helen and Polly in New York at a small political meeting in the Hotel Astor. Maury Maverick was
with us, just back from London, marvelling over the
skill of the English surgeons in the war. Vice-President
Truman had come up from Washington to make a short
speech, and we were all introduced to him. Later Helen
said, "He has an open hand. There are no crooks in his
fingers." She grasps character instantly. Truman was
deeply touched by Helen. He was in tears when she
spoke to him.

January, 1945

Helen writes that she has met F.D.R. in the White
House in a room with only his family about him. She
says, "Upon his worn face shines the heroic ambition of
Hercules to subdue the beasts of greed and deliver the
earth from robber states. . . . A mind-stretching spectacle
for us just emerging from pigmy chauvinism, is it not?"

She had witnessed the inauguration, standing with Jo
Davidson under the magnolia trees on the snow-covered
grounds of the White House, and during the reception
Jo, with his radiant grand manner, introduced Polly and
herself to high and low, to Attorney-General Francis

Biddle, Lord Halifax, various Senators and so on. With Jo she discussed between whiles the personages she was meeting and "the medley of hidden motives and influences out of which political movements spring."

In the evening of what she calls "that piled-up day," she dined with Justice Hugo Black, Thurman Arnold and others. They discussed the various roads by which Soviet Russia and the United States might reach genuine democracy, considering their conflicting views of economic determinism and conscious responsibility.

Helen writes again that she and Polly are "travelling fast from one government hospital to another," and she speaks of "the epic through which Polly and I are living. It is an epic beside which all Iliads and Æneids fade astonishingly. [Walt Whitman, in the Civil War hospitals, made a similar remark.] Everywhere on the tour we have seen extensive works of rehabilitation that had not been wrought before in history. Hospitals which would once have been valleys of the shadow . . . men facing an appalling diversity of infirmities and obstacles resolved to wring from them usefulness, self-reliance, yes, and even gaiety . . . You divine too the nervous tension we endured, the unshed tears, the need to be ever ready with encouragement as billow upon billow from the global anguish swept over us. But the upsurging message was worth all the pain to me."

Helen adds, regarding the hospitals, "Another miracle which electrified me was the coöperative organization by which the highest skills of surgery, medicine, teaching and the ingenuity of science are blended in a mag-

nificent endeavour to help multitudes of disabled
servicemen to regain their human heritage. Such a circu-
lation of fresh ideas and such an awakening of dormant
faculties will, I am sure, tend to place the handicapped in
the vanguard of civilization."

A letter from Helen, written in Thomasville, Georgia.
She had received at Charleston the news of Franklin
Roosevelt's death. She was in a gathering at the naval
hospital when Rear-Admiral James was called to the
telephone. When he announced that the President had
just died, "the company," she says, "went mute and limp,"
remembering that the purpose of his life had been "to
recast world society in liberty and decency." Helen adds,
"What a sombre prospect this must open up of unfulfilled
projects, constructive policies endangered, momentous
issues trembling in the balance. It is an irreplaceable void
we workers for the handicapped feel now that the tangi-
ble tokens of his sympathy and counsel are withdrawn.
My hospital visits have lost an indefinable something
which buoyed me up while he was among us."

August

I asked Helen what she thought of Booker T. Washington, whose *Up from Slavery* I have been reading. She
had spoken at Tuskegee and admired the founder for his
practical shrewdness and skill, but the Negro whom she
most venerates is Dr. George Washington Carver, a magnificent human being, as she calls him. To her he was
"Christlike in his unworldliness," refusing a vast salary
and giving the results of his experiments freely to all.

(He had extracted three hundred products from the pea-
nut and one hundred from the sweet potato.) Helen
reveres him as a combination of the scientist and the
saint.

In Helen's mind all races exist together, and this is
what W. E. Burghardt Du Bois hoped would prove to be
the case when, as a young student, he saw her at the
Perkins Institution. She was a child at the time, and he
had accompanied William James, his professor at Harvard. Hoping that she would be "blind to colour differences," Du Bois had followed her career, and he had not
been surprised when she spoke out frankly in Alabama
against what she called the iniquity of the colour line. It
was at a public meeting in Selma, and a Negro-baiter
asked Helen if she had given money for the defence of
Negroes. When she answered "Yes," he asked her further,
"Do you believe in marriage between whites and Negroes?"
To this she replied. "No more than they do." Then she
refused to shake hands with the man, for "I saw at
once what he was," she said to me this afternoon. She
shocked her own family, along with the other Alabamians,
but "They have forgotten it," she added.

When, as a child in Alabama, she was out with her
teacher and her Negro nurse, Anne Sullivan had refused
to accept ice cream in some public place because they
would not serve the Negro girl.

Polly described to me their visit to the Federal leper
colony at Carrville, Louisiana. Helen likes to touch people, her only way of getting into relation with them, and
here touching was forbidden. The lepers had been in-

structed to clasp their hands behind their backs as they
approached, and Helen was delighted when one young
man broke ranks and touched her. An older man, in his
room alone,—a very advanced case,—said he had known
Helen's brother in Texas. She told him they were on
their way to spend Thanksgiving Day with this brother
and she would tell him about their meeting. But the
man said, "Oh, no, he wouldn't know me." The reason
was that he had changed his name. Many lepers do this
in order not to disgrace their families, for, being often
ignorant people who think of leprosy in terms of the
Bible, they accept the idea that they are "unclean." As
it turned out, however, this was an educated man and
Phillips Keller really knew him.

Of the visitors' book at Carrville, Helen said that it
contained few names of outsiders who had been there.
But one whose name she found was Ruth Draper.

September

Today, more than usually, an air of Scotland pervades
Arcan Ridge,—named after an old farmhouse in the
Scottish Highlands,—and Polly Thomson, who has been
with Helen since 1914, speaks with a livelier than ever
Scottish accent. For this evening William Allan Neilson
comes to dinner, the president of Smith College who was
one of Helen's professors at Radcliffe and learned the
manual alphabet to talk with her there. Neilson still
speaks broad Scots, almost every word "with hair on it,"
as Rudolph Ruzicka said of another Scotsman.

After dinner there was some talk about Polly's Dram-
buie, a kind of chartreuse that Bonnie Prince Charlie

gratefully sent back from France as a gift to the Scots.
Then the talk fell on Scottish songs. Helen went upstairs
to her study,—for she knows her way perfectly about the
house,—and brought down a two-volume collection of
Scottish songs in braille which the publishers in Edinburgh had sent her. She read the table of contents with
her fingers rapidly, found a song she wanted, turned the
pages and read it out to us,—a Highland "wail from
Skye," as Polly put it.

With Helen and Polly to the harvest festival at the
Jewish Theological Seminary far up-town in New York.
Midday meal in the sukkah, the festival tent set up in the
quadrangle. The walls were hung with the fruits of the
season, or all the fruits of the Holy Land that are men-
tioned in the Bible. We sat with the president of the
Seminary, Dr. Louis Finkelstein, and the famous Hebrew
scholar Dr. Samuel Lieberman. Helen surprised these
great Jewish doctors with her knowledge of the Bible. I
remembered her remark that she had read her braille
Bible until whole pages of dots had been rubbed off.

Listening to the Hebrew grace with her fingers on Dr.
Finkelstein's lips, she said, "This is the rhythm of life.
It is like the voice of the Lord upon many waters, the
Lord of Glory thundering."

Then she said, "The Bible is the only book that reaches
up to the times in which we live. It speaks with knowledge of the sun, the skies, the sea and the beauty of
distant stars . . . There are no differences in men. Differences are only as the variations in shadows cast by the
sun."

Of Dr. Finkelstein's Conference on Science, Philosophy and Religion, she said, "It is human brotherhood starting, and how I wish to see it coming. This is the cornerstone and we must see to it that the cornerstone is not rejected.

After lunch we rode downtown in a Broadway bus to the Grand Central Station. Helen likes to feel the crowd around her. Suddenly she said, "There is a painter in the bus." I looked around and, sure enough, there was a house-painter sitting in a corner at the other end of the bus, twenty feet away.

I remembered an evening in a certain restaurant where Jo Davidson had taken us all to dinner. At the end of ten minutes Helen knew more than any of us about the people who were sitting at the neighbouring tables. She knew them from their perfume, the kind of soap they used, the quality of their cigar smoke, even the dishes they had ordered. From these elements she built up a true picture of them.

July, 1946

Dinner at Helen's. She was up at five, as usual this summer, clipping the borders. Then, after making her bed, she always runs down the ramp from her door and goes out for her walk. She follows the hand-rail that Polly calls "Helen's walk" and that twists its way through the woods and curves back to the house.

"Helen says,"—how often Polly has uttered these words, interpreting for me, for I have not learned properly how to talk with Helen. I remember the feeling of shock when I first met her. How could one ever cross that gulf and get into communication with her? But in a moment one forgot her disabilities and entered a wonderful world of happiness and wisdom.

Helen says she agrees with Bacon in preferring young men to old because of their inventiveness and courage.

Helen is ready for any adventure. We talked about the gypsies and Konrad Bercovici, and I told her how Bercovici took me through the East Side one night where the gypsies were camping out in the cellars of old warehouses. Obliged to come into the city so that their children could go to school, they lived in these abandoned cellars just as they lived on the road in summer. They even set up tents and built campfires on the concrete floors, while their young women told fortunes on the streets.

Helen was all excitement as Polly translated this into her hand. She asked me to remind Bercovici of his promise to take her through the East Side and show her the gypsies.

October, 1947

To lunch with Helen and Polly. They took possession of their new house ten days ago. Since the fire it has been rebuilt, and Helen's friends in Japan have filled it with new gifts to replace those that were burned a year ago. The rooms are furnished with inlaid tables, lamps, trays, boxes, chests, Satsuma pieces, ornaments by the greatest ceramist in Japan, carved ivory figures, prints, an imperial picnic kit of lacquer and gold, gifts from a Shinto priest and an incense-burner, inlaid with gold and silver, presented by the Emperor of Japan. If all these objects had not been so charmingly and humanly arranged by Polly, one might almost think the house a Japanese museum.

But what a calamity was the fire of November, 1946. From the burned house nothing was saved except the silver, which had been removed, or nothing but a few scattered sheets, picked up, half burned, in the meadow, of Helen's unfinished long poem of 1912. In this she had undertaken to compare her own life-experience with that of the workers, as she had supposed this to be in her early socialist days. All her treasures were destroyed when the house was burned to the ground,—her braille library, her letters and papers and the three-quarters finished book that she was writing about her teacher. She had worked on this in spare moments during many years, accumulating a mass of notes, all of them copied and sorted. Already she is planning to write this book again, but when will she ever have the time to do it? Her unceasing practical work has brought her a sense of responsibility and an anxiety to meet it with flying colours. Only her early morning walks when she is at home bring her carefree hours for this kind of thinking.

When, in Rome, she heard the news, her own feeling of disaster was instantly lost in a sense of the magnitude of the woes of others. She writes that she at once felt "life triumphant over the narrowness of my bodily existence . . . This inner life surged and expanded within me, and I marvelled at the security I felt in my spiritual home."

XI

AROUND THE WORLD

UNLIKE THE MAJORITY OF THE BLIND, who are apt to fail earlier than those who see, and are even supposed to die earlier in life, Helen Keller, with every year, seemed to grow more vigorous as she continually extended the scope of her work. When the second world war coiled itself about her mind, she felt a mountain of suffering laid upon her, for in much of the world the condition of the blind,—her own special charge,—was almost more calamitous than it ever had been. Many of their homes had been destroyed, their hard-won schools and workshops had been wrecked or looted by the Nazis, their braille plates were melted down for ammunition and countless braille books had been burned for fuel. Helen Keller, in her journeys through England, France, Italy and Greece, everywhere talking to blinded soldiers and sailors, as well as to women and children blinded by bombs, must have concluded with Bertrand Russell that the sum of human misery had never been as great as it was during this time. Moreover,—to consider the blind alone,—what was to be said of those of the non-European peoples? In the ten years that followed the war, Helen Keller, in the interest of the

144

blind, visited Australia, South America, Africa and
Asia. She might have taken as her motto Theodore
Roethke's line, "I learn by going where I have to
go."

Meanwhile, before the end of the war, she had begun
to visit the naval and army hospitals in her own country, starting in Washington and stopping at seventy
or more from Arkansas to Oregon, through the East
and the South. She was hesitant at first because of
her imperfect speech and what she regarded as her
clumsiness and slowness, but she performed in the
end, as many were to testify, what would have passed
for miracles in less case-hardened ages. She, too, blind
and deaf, relived the war in her imagination as she
passed from hospital room to room, talking to the
blinded and deafened young men whose hands pulsed
with emotion, with irrepressible humour and responsive courage. She crept through the tropical jungles
with them, strained over mountains, marched over the
desert, traversed the cold wastes of the north Atlantic,
crouched with them in a world of smoke and dust
and dreadful sounds as fighter planes dropped bombs
that shook the earth. Many of their hands, aquiver
with thought and meant for violins rather than guns,
were pitifully defaced by burns, mutilated, twisted;
and they struck her somehow as trails crossing her palm
that stood for a vast migration from one era to another.
Homesickness on such a scale had perhaps never been
seen before, and more than ever she was glad of the

years she had journeyed back and forth through the cities and along the rivers of Walt Whitman's country. For it was such a pleasure for the men to hear someone speak of the places they knew with Whitman's kind of human imagination. "You are a marine," she would say to one, knowing from his muscles, knotted and tense, that he had had a marine's rigorous training, while the shoulder muscles of a sailor were usually, to her touch, smooth and relaxed. Like the "wound-dresser" of the Civil War, she loved their healthy-mindedness, together with their valiant efforts to retrieve their lives.

At intervals of a year or two, she set out, in the meantime, for Australia, for New Zealand and, again, Japan, for South America later on, for Cape Town and Johannesburg, for Egypt, the proverbial "country of the blind." There, in Cairo, two or three months before the republic was declared, she was struck by the prodigious energy with which this country had roused itself from its more than millennial slumber, while she found herself obliged to make a new kind of speech, addressing Mohammedan university students and professors. With the prime minister, a philosopher and poet, she was able to talk Plato, who had meant so much to her in her own life, while she convinced the minister of education that more schools should be opened for the blind. Visiting between-whiles the schools at Alexandria and Aboukir, she read history with her hands in Oriental carvings till her

fingers were drunk, as she said, with the endless
variety that she felt on every wall and door. She was
driven out to spend a night on the desert in a bunga-
low in the shadow of the pyramids, under the stars,
where she felt, stretching out in every direction over
the sands, an immense silence hostile to life and
growth. In the waste air swaying out to her she was
aware of a stillness the dread meaning of which she
could not fathom until she began to remember the
revolting accounts she had read as a girl of the ani-
mistic faiths and oppressions of ancient Egypt. She
recalled the tales of the building of the pyramids when
multitudes of human beings had groaned and died in
order that the bodies of the pharaohs might be pre-
served, and she shuddered as she realized how the
slaves had journeyed from the Nile under the lash,
dragging huge blocks of granite over the sands. She
could feel the ropes of the sledges cutting their flesh.
She recalled the revenues that were wrung from the
people for sacrifices to the souls of the deified kings,
souls more akin to crocodiles than to mankind, and
she felt that the silence of the desert was a retributive
silence.

No more than for Schweitzer was it easy for her to
see good in the future or to believe in progress quite
as of old when even the bitterest of modern thinkers
had not envisaged the ruin that was to befall the
twentieth century world. But in Egypt she realized
vividly, as Breasted had realized a few decades before,

that civilization was only a half-hour old, that the world had been somewhat civilized only, as it were, overnight and man was still pathetically young and simple. He was bewildered by forces he had not yet learned to control, and Helen Keller could also see, what her earlier impatience had failed to perceive, that all the important ideas are slow in growing. Knowing that, as Breasted said, the epoch of conscience and character began only five thousand years ago,— as datable an event as the introduction of metal,—she too could see that progress was demonstrable historically, like Breasted's "unconquerable buoyancy of the human soul." She could see this in the Arab lands, Lebanon, Syria, Jordan, struggling with colossal social problems and willing to listen when she spoke of the blind who have minds that can be developed as well as hands that can be trained. How much more in Israel, with its hopeful cheer and energy, where the great Bible associations seemed to have inspired a burning force in some of the descendants of the prophets. She studied the tremendous irrigation projects, watching the people breaking up rocks and stones to free the soil and reap the first harvest in two thousand years. She could see the bread of future generations in the young trees and the delicate green of the wheat. There, too, as everywhere she went, schools for the blind rose as she passed, while she could share with Ben-Gurion her devotion to Plato.

In all these countries Helen Keller was able to

read the signs of the times, she understood what was
happening everywhere, and, always eager to meet the
minds of Arabs, Jews and Japanese, she comprehended
their needs and aspirations. Moreover, she spoke
for the deep America that politicians misrepresent,
moulded as her own outlook was by the planetary-
minded Emerson and Whitman whom so many Asians
had taken for the American prophets. She carried
their ideas to South America,—Chile, Brazil, Peru,—
as well as to South Africa, where a thought followed
her like a reproach, the thought of race-intolerance
and its meanness and folly. Dreaming of a great fra-
ternity of races governed by justice and reason, she
felt that toleration was the greatest of the gifts of the
mind. On the voyage to Cape Town she walked at
night on the upper deck while Polly described the
Southern Cross above them,—a constellation that
for her symbolized consciousness flashing out of darkness and the unknown. Then at dawn Polly also
described how thick clouds put obstacles in the path
of the sun as it laboured up the sky. In the comfort-
ing shelter of the ship, Helen Keller thought again
of the horror of blindness falling on a man, so that he
felt like a castaway in the open sea. But what real
security had she herself ever known,—or, for that
matter, what had she ever desired? Perhaps because
of her insecurity life had always retained for her what
she called the "urgent poignancy of a crisis . . . the
sense of crisis which," as she observed in *Let Us Have*

Faith, "pulls the faculties to a point and intensifies action." What harm had been done to the present generation by the feeling that it could live serene in a more or less permanent order of things! It had expected stability and found none either without or within; it was staggered by apocalyptic events and wrecked illusions.

She had always associated Africa with tremendous adventures, while ever since she and her teacher had read *The Story of an African Farm* she had connected this country with tragedy also. As a spur for her courage, as she approached it, she read the life of Mahatma Gandhi, who had known so well its racial problems and who, ignoring the evil in people, had often succeeded in changing them by regarding them as they wished to be, not as they were. The miracles he had performed had sprung from his faith in human nature, a faith that was very like her own, for she was astonished not by its faults but by the strength with which men had risen, whenever they had previously fallen, through the ages. Alan Paton shared this faith,—the author of *Cry, the Beloved Country* who had heard of Helen Keller when he was a schoolboy, excited by the wondrous tale of this victim of fate who had opened all doors by one creative step after another. He wrote a preface for *Helen Keller Under the Southern Cross* after her two months' tour appealing for the blind, when the halls had been so crowded and the papers had been so full of her that

she was the centre of interest in the whole country.
She won the young especially, in Durban, in Johannesburg, in the little sand-blown villages with their
ox-carts and donkeys, where she noted that most of
the village crafts were suited to the blind,—leather-
work, pottery, mat-making, basketry, weaving. One
had only to train the blind in these occupations, and
for this no special teachers were required. Meanwhile,
in the midst of her race with engagements, this lover
of animals and zoos enjoyed a brief holiday in Kruger
National Park, driving all day among giraffes, zebras,
lions, ostriches and herds of deer with antlers shaped
like lyres. In the land of the Afrikanders, as in other
countries, she left hospitals and schools that bore her
name; and there again she became a symbol of what
Tolstoy called "the religious perception of our time."
For, as Tolstoy said, in every period there exists an
understanding of the meaning of life, defining the
highest good at which the period aims, and in our
time this consists in "the acknowledgement that the
aim of life is the union of mankind."

One of Helen Keller's tours took her to southern
Greece, to visit the war-stricken blind, in 1946; and,
heartsick as she was there, she felt she could not leave
without at least a glimpse of the Parthenon. Before
beginning the ascent, she searched among the ruins
till she found a fallen pillar of the temple of Zeus,
and this she examined from end to end, measuring
its diameter, so that she might imagine how the

columns of the Parthenon looked. It was a toilsome climb up rough steps and slipping stones, but this counted for nothing when she reached the summit and touched the pillars which the elements and time had failed to ravage. In the distance lay Salamis, and, close by, the Agora where the Athenians gathered when the fleet-footed runners brought the good news from Marathon, the spots where they listened to the counsels of Pericles and Socrates taught the young men and Euripides raised his voice in compassion for mankind. Many other associations of Helen Keller's childhood flooded through her mind as she stood on the height. In the midst of this triumph of the ancient architects and engineers, the myths and poems she had known came back to life, with Anne Sullivan's tales of the siege of Troy and the games in which teacher and pupil had so often taken the parts of barbarian and Greek. She felt the serene atmosphere in which Pallas Athene moved and men had received visits from the gods, and she realized once more how far these Greek associations had gone to form her own mind and her own spirit.

XII

A LATER MISCELLANY

October, 1949

This evening one of our friends asked Helen how
she had come to understand abstractions. She said she
had found that good apples were sweet and that there
were also bad apples that were bitter. Then she learned
to think of the sweetness and bitterness apart from the
apples. She grasped the idea of sweetness and bitterness
in themselves. Sir Alfred Zimmern, at dinner with us,
my friend since the days when he wrote *The Greek
Commonwealth* forty years ago, exclaimed as he listened
to Helen, "She is exactly following the method of
Plato." And indeed her words and their rhythm were
Platonic.

Christmas, 1951

Helen has a way of bursting out at table with the
most surprising remarks. Today she was full of Thucydides, whose history she has been reading this Christmas
morning. She talked about the Peloponnesian war.
"What a stupid war!—the stupidest war in history,"
she said, shaking her head in mournful disapproval. She
had been brooding and grieving over this war, which
destroyed the democracy of Athens. For the rest, she was
sure there was nothing about war that Thucydides did
not know.

153

The other day she suddenly spoke of a certain Evelyn
Chessman, an English entomologist who had written wonderful things about insects. Helen may have read her in
one of the braille magazines, whether English, American,
German or French, for she keeps up with them all.

Polly took her up. "What's this, Helen? Who is this
Evelyn Chessman?" Polly likes to tease her, and she is
sometimes severe with her. For instance, if Helen makes
a mistake in typewriting one of her letters, Polly makes
her copy the page again. Usually Helen's typing is like
an expert stenographer's, but the other day there were
a few dim lines in one of her letters and she added this
postscript: "Polly says the writing of this machine doesn't
please her critical eye. My apologies. H.K."

To return to the lady entomologist, Helen is charmingly eager about these shining bits of knowledge. She
has the earnest innocence of a ten-year-old child. She
says rightly in one of her books: "The wonder and
imaginative freshness of childhood have never withered
in my breast." Moreover, having read only, or mainly,
all her life, the great books, her mind remains singularly
uncorrupted. She is a standing rebuke to those for whom
"sophistication," that dubious and ambiguous quality, is
the sum of all goods.

There are times when she speaks like an oracle or an
Asiatic sage, for she perfectly carries out the injunction
to man in Melville's *Moby Dick* to "live in the world
without being of it." In spite of her incessant work,
much of her life is still spent in solitary meditation,
alone in the dark with her own thoughts, or with the

Bible or the Greek poets, and, as she lives in her way as the old prophets lived in the desert, many of her words inspire a kind of reverential wonder. She naturally uses archaic and poetic expressions of the sort that children pick up in their reading, words that are seldom heard in the ordinary talk that she rarely hears except when the ever-alert Polly passes it on to her.

(Wonderful in her way is Polly also. Without her vitality, her tact and her feeling for the drama of life, what would Helen do in her journeys about the world? And what an inexhaustible buoyancy both of them have! I have seen them together on a midnight train when everyone else was asleep or nodding while they smiled and chatted like birds on a branch in the morning.)

February, 1952

In a corner of the lawn at Helen's house stands a Japanese stone lantern, nine feet high. It is a seventeenth century piece, a gift of Yamanaka, and it now contains a lamp that is always kept burning. Polly says this is to symbolize the "unquenchable spirit of Helen Keller."

Helen showed me a list of books that she had drawn up, hoping they might all be put into braille, and I saw that she had included Wendell Phillips's speeches. This was the orator who championed all the underdogs, a friend of Dr. Howe's at the Perkins Institution, and it struck me that Helen, in her way,—child of the deep South that she is,—has carried on the line of the old Boston reformers. I had observed that sometimes in speaking she breaks into a kind of oratory that vaguely suggests to me the abolitionist tradition, the tradition of

William Lloyd Garrison in which John Jay Chapman grew up, like O. G. Villard and like Roger Baldwin later. She is also, after all, a child of the circle of Dr. Howe, although she knew little of its general interests until years after she had left it.

She has been reading in braille Amiel's Journal, which my son and I translated years ago, and the other evening she spoke of this with both admiration and indignation. He had referred to Jews in a way that she could not forgive, and today she writes to me about this as follows:

"Amiel's Journal interests me especially first because he reminds me of Teacher. It is true, he was timid while she was recklessly courageous, but he resembled her in many respects,—her nervous temperament, her impatience with the hopeless stupidity of the world, her consuming love of beauty both in nature and in human beings. He too developed a large charity that enabled him to conquer the resentment and the vindictive feelings he had towards people who had evidently treated him harshly. He suffered much from his eyes like Teacher, and he also shrank from old age."

Helen goes on to say that she will "treasure the Journal as a work of the ages," continuing, "Whenever my mind dries up for want of expression, I will go to Amiel's magnificent reservoir of ideas for inspiration." But there was a passage in which in 1877 he wrote like a common anti-Semite, and it was this that horrified her. For how many fine Jews she had known and loved as friends and as helpers in her work! Moreover, she says, "It was plain

to me that Amiel had not read the Old Testament carefully, or he would not have characterized the prophets
by implication as the spokesmen of a narrow despotic
God, 'a partial and vigilant pedagogue who proceeds
only by particular cases and not by universal rules.' How
this idea runs counter to my readings of Isaiah, Hosea,
Micah and Amos and what I have learned about Hillel
and Maimonides!"

I have just read that H. G. Wells, on his last visit
to this country, called Helen Keller "the most wonderful
being in America." How many times that has been said
since the days of Mark Twain and of Oliver Wendell
Holmes earlier still. Another English traveller compared
her a few years ago, as one of the world's wonders, with
the falls of Niagara.

What aspect of her life and character do these ob-
servers have in mind? Her adventurousness, perhaps,
or her powers of intuitive or physical perception. Once,
flying over the mountains of West Virginia, she asked
the pilot if they were not at an altitude of 8000 feet.
The pilot reported afterwards that he looked at his
instruments and found that they showed an altitude of
8000 feet exactly. Now, deaf and blind as she is, she
has piloted a plane. She was on her way from Rome
to London and the pilot, Captain Lamb, had asked her
to sit in the cockpit. Then, while the plane was flying
over Corsica, he offered her the wheel. "I could easily
perceive the motions up and down, back and forth,
from side to side," she wrote later, "as I steered for

several minutes." She added, characteristically, that she
could see what flying cost the pilot in alertness and
fatigue.

I asked Polly when and how she and Helen had first
met their great friend Katharine Cornell. It was in the
thirties on a train from Boston. The train was lurching
and they were laughing as they struggled towards the
dining-car, and there was Katharine Cornell waiting to
receive them.

Once in a while Polly wishes to go to a matinée all
by herself, and on these rare occasions she leaves Helen
in Katharine Cornell's dressing-room. Helen always brings
with her some book in braille to read, and Katharine
Cornell comes in between the acts and tells her the news
of the theatre and her own play. She is the only person
with whom Polly ever leaves Helen entirely alone.

Helen has received as a Christmas present from some
unknown friend in Japan a mountain roller, a singing
bird, that arrived by plane. It is one of the few birds
she has had as pets. But ever since her childhood, birds,
though unseen, have remained for her as much a part
of her world as stones and flowers. Her teacher had kept
some pigeons in a cage so that when they were let out
Helen could chase them and learn about their flight and
the beauty of wings.

June, 1952

Helen is in Paris for the centenary of the death of
Louis Braille, the most famous character in all the

history of the blind. A pupil in the school of Haüy, he found this teacher's system of raised letters too difficult and cumbersome, and he made it possible for the blind to write with comparative ease and read what they had written. A village saddler's son, he became an organist in Paris and what Helen calls "the Gutenberg of the blind."

With members of Braille's family, she was present at the Pantheon when his ashes were deposited there with those of the poets, philosophers and statesmen of France. She had paid tribute to him at the Sorbonne, thanking the authorities for recognizing "the spirit and efforts of all who refuse to succumb to limitations." She was made a Chevalier of the Legion of Honour. "She spoke in heavily accented but faultlessly grammatical French," Florence Davidson writes after the ceremony. "Standing before the audience, she was radiant and the applause was thunderous."

Helen's interest in poetry is inexhaustible. She has read a little of Auden but not much, and she once wrote, "He has not the vocabulary to distinguish the fire of heaven from the fire of earth, so he uses his metre to indicate the difference." When she asked me about him, I tried to tell her about his wit, his technical originality and his feeling for the time-spirit.

Polly feels that no one can ever appreciate Helen enough, and she was delighted by something I passed on to her. One of our neighbours was standing the other day on a corner of Park Avenue in New York. A taxi drove up and, stopped by a red light, the chauffeur called out, "Lady, I have just driven Helen Keller!" He could not contain his excitement, neither could Polly contain her pleasure in the story.

What a privilege it is to know such generous beings. Greatest of all is the pleasure of knowing that Helen Keller actually is what simple people think she is, a reality that can withstand the coldest eye.

Helen has just returned from a call on President Eisenhower. She has been received by eight previous presidents. This time she regrets that she did not find out the names of the trees in the grounds of the White House.

June, 1953

Helen is seventy-three years old today. She lives much in eternity and much in history, but she only lives in time when she is able to keep up with the news. This week she returned from a two-months' absence in South America, and she has not had a moment yet to catch up with the newspapers and magazines. Unable to talk politics, she talks at table about Pepys's diary, which our host Stuart Grummon is reading. She fishes up two or three facts about Pepys that we had forgotten or never known, remembered from her own reading thirty years ago.

What variety there is in her mind! She is interested in everything. One day she recalled to me the dancing of La Argentina. Another day she quoted at length from a new fine poem of Robinson Jeffers, who told me once that he had seen her name in the register of a hotel in the Orkney islands. And what happy phrases

come to her mind. When some children spelled words
into her hand with their small fingers, she said they
were like "the wild flowers of conversation."

Today Polly took us up to Helen's study and opened
the door without first warning her that we were coming.
Polly turned on the light. Helen, sitting in the dark,—
for the light meant nothing to her,—had a look of
seraphic happiness such as I had never seen on a human
countenance. It suggested to me the *samâdhi,* the ecstasy,
of the Hindus, or that highest rapture which the practice of orison is said to produce as a result of the
methodical elevation of the soul. I recalled an incident
in the life of Emanuel Swedenborg, recounted by Signe
Toksvig in her biography. When Swedenborg was on
shipboard once, a Danish general entered his cabin un-
announced. Swedenborg was seated with his elbows on
the table, his hands supporting his face. His eyes were
open and "much elevated," the general said, for he was
in a state of ecstasy, a trance. "When addressed, he rose
with some confusion and advanced with a singular and
visible uncertainty," but, as the general concluded, he
"soon recovered." The general might have been describing Helen Keller this afternoon as she gradually returned
to the world we live in.

I thought of Helen when I read the colonel's soliloquy
at the end of Arthur Koestler's *The Age of Longing.* He
observed that American women are all too busy "playing
bridge" to be "cut out for the part of martyrs and
saints . . . American womanhood," the colonel went on,

"has produced no Maids of Orleans, no Rosa Luxembourgs or Madame Curies, no Brontës or Florence Nightingales or Krupskayas"; and one might add that it seldom produces anyone as rash as various people who generalize about it. For how many types there are in our teeming population! One might easily suggest a list to set beside the list this fictional colonel has drawn up from three or four countries. The names of Dorothea Lynde Dix, Emily Dickinson, Jane Addams would appear somewhere on such a list, and I dare say that for not a few the name of Helen Keller would figure as leading all the rest.

CODA

Helen comes to see us, bringing for our new house a large red and black lacquered Japanese bowl. The God of Laughter is painted on the rounded cover. If Helen were a polytheist, this would be one of her favourite gods, for none of her traits is more marked than her sense of humour. A biographer of Gandhi says that he grew gayer all the time, the more he reconciled in himself the elements of life: as he "progressively established harmony in place of discrepancy, he became happy, relaxed and gay." So it seems to be with Helen Keller. The older she grows the sadder,—and the gayer,—she is.

So I wrote in October, 1949. Let me continue now as follows:

There is nothing Helen Keller dislikes more than what she calls "the flowery compliments to me as a 'goddess' or a 'saint'"; and she has written somewhere that she is "sickened by the unthinking adulation bestowed upon" her. But in this matter of gaiety the saints have been generally like her. I do not mean certain saints who are fashionable nowadays, for one, the cheerless creature in *The Cocktail Party*. Nor does she resemble the much talked of Simone Weil for whom "unhappiness" was "the supreme evidence of God's love." Is not that an illustration of neuroticism rather than sainthood? William James was surely right when he spoke in *The Varieties of Religious Experience* of "the happiness which achieved religious belief confers." He adds, "There is an organic affinity between joyousness and tenderness," observing that the saints are "joyous and tender."

Much as she dislikes it, there is nothing new in the imputation of saintliness to Helen Keller. When she was young and living at Wrentham, a woman walked down to the lake to dip her hands in the water in which she had bathed; and, since I have quoted William James, I might go on to say that she has many of the characteristics he ascribes to saintliness. One is an "auroral openness" and "a feeling of being in a wider life than that of this world's selfish little interests . . . an immense elation and freedom, a shifting of the emotional centre towards loving and harmonious affections." The saints know nothing of those "cowardly obstructions which in tame persons and dull moments are sovereign impediments to action," borne as they are "on a tide of love, indignation, generosity, magnanimity, admiration, loyalty or enthusiasm of self-surrender." Helen Keller has illustrated James's thesis in *The Energies of Men* regarding what he called "the resources of the subliminal region," and like many of the saints she has combined a spiritual and mystical force with an indomitable energy in practical matters. It was James himself who wrote to her when she was a young girl,

"The sum and substance of it is that you are a blessing." If he could see her gaiety now, amid all the suffering she has witnessed and shared, he might characterize her in the phrase of the Italian mystic: "The true monk takes nothing with him but his lyre."

Somewhere Helen Keller has written, answering the clever ones who think it is "noble and comely to be unhappy," that "Delight is essential to growth and self-improvement. Do not the pleasures of taste enable the body to assimilate food? What mind that thinks at all does not choose the ideas that please it and let all others go unheeded? . . . He who does not see that joy is an important force in the world misses the essence of life. Joy is a spiritual element that gives vicissitudes unity and significance. Belief in the triumph of good vitalizes a race; enlightened optimism fosters in man a constructive purpose and frees him from fears that fetter his thought."

What a response is that to David Reisman's statement that "pessimism has become an opiate" in our day! And what a response is Helen Keller to the smart blasphemers who sneer at "our neighbours' earthly welfare," as if this were merely materialistic, as if body and soul were not interrelated and misery were not an impediment to the growth of the spirit. Our fatalistic epoch, which has lost faith in the goodness of men, still recognizes the saints of the religion of art,—who are often in other respects mundane or vicious,—while it ignores the real saints who exist among us and remind us that human nature is not a snake-pit. But the fame of Albert Schweitzer shows what a hunger for goodness exists in the world, a hunger that many novels are now disclosing, with a belief that "goodness is the only value that seems . . . to have any claim to be an end in itself." It is Somerset Maugham who says this in *The Summing-Up,* and he adds what everybody feels in Helen Keller's presence: "When now and then I have come across real goodness I have found reverence rise naturally in my heart."